DEDICATION AND THANKS

To God, for my inspiration.
To my husband Neville, my biggest fan.
To sub-editor Yvonne Densem, who "got" me and this book.
To all of the other wonderful people I have met along the way
who have taught me so much.

Let's

YOUR JOURNEY

HEALTH AND WELLBEING

RELATIONSHIPS

LIVING HIGHER

Introduction

This book is not intended to tell you how to live your life or to make any judgement at all.

The expression of this book comes out of my own experience, learning, understanding, reading, listening, talking and living a very full life – all 50 years so far.

These expressions are from all aspects of my life – professional and personal. I am not sure why, but I live my life with such a sense of urgency, as if there is no tomorrow. It's been challenging at times, but I sure have been a lot of places, met a lot of people, done a lot of things and had many phenomenal experiences, so I have no regrets.

The intention of this book is to help you, the reader, pause and think carefully about how you are living your life; to figure out what's working for you and what's not; to identify your dreams and inspirations; to make choices that will take you to where you want to be, doing what you want to do and, most importantly, being who you are supposed to be.

So you too can say "I LOVE MY LIFE! I am living it well"

My heart's desire is for this book to express kindness and gentleness towards you – and in doing that, liberate you in some way.

May God bless you my friend, as He has blessed me, and even more so.

Heather B.

Each topic or segment is written in three sections:

1. Points to Consider
2. Personal Comment
3. Girltalk Challenge

••

The book allows you different ways to read it and
let it speak to you.

1. You can read it from cover to cover and let parts
   of it connect with you and help you consider your
   own view or feelings.

2. You can pick and choose a topic you wish to read
   from time to time, as a refresher or reminder.

3. You can fully engage in the book section by section,
   week by week and allow the material to work changes
   in you as you consider each topic and participate in
   the Girltalk Challenges.

••

The Girltalk Challenges don't necessarily take much of
your time. The challenges are designed to stimulate a
positive shift in your thinking and attitudes. Physically
putting the challenge into action will cement a change of
thinking and attitude deep within you. In addition, when
you undertake the Girltalk Challenges, I feel sure you will
begin to see rewards appear in your life.

**You will get out of it what you put in and MORE.
The choice is yours.**

Your
Journey

SEA OF HOPE

The next wave will be one of Hope

Enjoy the journey of life

Many of life's questions will always remain unanswered to most of us. I spent a great deal of time trying to figure everything out, so once I had, I could get on with 'enjoying my life'. Now, at the age of 50, I realise I am never going to achieve that. What a lot of precious time I wasted.

But on the positive side, I can now get on with enjoying the journey, learning as I go and having heaps of fun along the way. It sure feels good to finally come to that place. Maybe the following things will help you truly enjoy the journey of your life.

Make the most of each special moment and each day, as often as you can, pause and acknowledge each moment that is precious to you. Hold it, extend it and remember it. Remember to live in each moment. We all need reminding to do this because we rush our lives away, forgetting "THIS IS MY LIFE" and it will be over all too soon.

Come to the place of knowing 'life is a journey' to be enjoyed step by step. Don't be in a hurry to be somewhere else, enjoy now. None of us wants to get to the end of this life and be full of regrets.

If you had the opportunity to go to the end of your life and look back, to see a life you would be proud of and happy with, what would you be looking at that is not currently in your present life? What changes would you make to ensure the things you want to look back on are included in your life?

Make a list of these things and add them to your life plan. Life is to be enjoyed as you go, otherwise you will get to the end and will have missed it. Do what you need to do to enjoy your journey called LIFE. Please, make that list.

Do not miss your life. Continue to enjoy the journey through good and bad times, learning, loving and laughing as you go. When the bad times come, dig deep, press on, pick yourself up and keep going. You will get through it - and most times, be stronger and wiser. Try not to let the difficult times stall you, keep moving. I want to say that again – "Keep moving."

Life is to be celebrated as you go, you know this deep in your heart. Make sure you remind yourself of this regularly. Drink more champagne (in moderation, of course).

Each day of the journey brings a new opportunity of enjoyment. You are responsible for enjoying the journey of your life; no one else can do this for you. Enjoying your journey doesn't necessarily come naturally, but developing a positive attitude about yourself and living with a heart of thankfulness will help you enjoy your journey. Live the 'Best Life' as you go.

Your life is a moment by moment journey. Stay connected to the little moments; that's the real life journey.

Personal Comment:

I don't believe the destination is the enjoyment. No, every day can be enjoyed! Learn how to 'extend the moment', capture and savour it. It's in the moments of the journey you will find the real joy.

I love the thought of taking a moment and Holding it…Extending it… Capturing it…Savouring it…Remembering it. Practise this and you will understand what I mean.

Since I learnt how to do this, my enjoyment level has certainly risen. Now it's become a habit I practise almost all of the time. I am in the second half of my life and have made a choice to try not to miss any more moments and opportunities to enjoy my life. I have found a bonus of this is finding joy in almost everything. Yes, I do drink more champagne! (One glass at a time, of course.)

Heather says
"Enjoy the Moments of the Journey"

GIRLTALK CHALLENGE

Stop and take a moment out of your day. Any moment will do and take a few seconds to fully engage in that moment.

Hold it …
Extend it …
Capture it …
Savour it …
Remember it.

Practise doing this regularly and develop it into a habit. Your enjoyment level will increase greatly. Go on – do it, you will love it!

It is truly a wonderful way to engage in the beautiful moments called YOUR LIFE. My desire for you is that you will truly enjoy your journey.

G

THE DANCE OF MY SOUL

It is most joyous when you find the place of allowing your soul to dance

You can choose a great life

Our life is a series of choices and decisions we make each and every day. Some people are not aware of the full extent to which daily choices affect their life and their future.

We are given a free will to make life creating choices. Much of what we choose is determined by our attitudes, our beliefs and what we believe we are worthy of. What are we choosing at present? What will we choose for our future? Each decision, large and small contributes to the outcome of our life.

At every crossroad, or point of decision making, we are faced with choices (and there are many, almost daily).

- Choose wisely - always choose the High Road to a greater life. Know the High Road is seldom the easy road. Know the Power of Choice is in your own hands.
- A series of wise choices will bring positive results – a series of unwise choices produces negative results.
- Wherever you are now, you can begin a series of wise choices to start you on your journey to a wonderful life. I have discovered this in my own life.
- It is never too late to begin. Are you prepared to make the appropriate changes? You are worthy of the very best life.
- Choose a GREAT life.

DEFINITION:

Great[1] - unusual or considerable in degree, power, intensity; wonderful; first-rate; very good; notable; remarkable; exceptionally outstanding; important; highly significant or consequential.

- Be wary of becoming impatient. Making good choices consistently will pay off in the end. It's a journey. The little daily decisions and choices do contribute to our future; don't underestimate even the smallest of decisions, or believe these things to be so small they are insignificant. Remember all the little things will contribute to the difference in the end. For example:
  - Choosing to re-educate yourself
  - Choosing to forgive and let go
  - Choosing to be a giver
  - Choosing to look after your Body, Soul, Spirit
  - Choosing the partner you can share your life with, who enhances who you are and vice versa.
  - Choosing the right time for marriage
  - Choosing when to have children
  - Choosing when to travel
  - Choosing when to invest
  - Choosing when to make major life-altering changes
  - Choosing when to be still and wait
  - Choosing to eat well and exercise
  - Choosing to be grateful every day
  - Choosing a positive attitude – and many more.

Wise choices take extra time, effort, energy, focus, patience, discretion; but all these things give you a greater reward. The wonderful thing about the power and opportunity of choice is it is open for negotiation at all times.

Consider carefully all the facts and history when making life choices. Apply wisdom, knowledge, experience, understanding, common sense and insight.

DEFINITION:
Wisdom[2] - The ability to discern or judge what is true, right or lasting. Insight; The quality or state of being wise; knowledge of what is true or right. Common sense; good judgement.

66

Personal Comment:

A few years ago I suddenly 'got it' – the power of my own choices and how I can and do choose my own life, my experiences, my relationships and therefore my future.

It was an exhilarating moment for me, realising the power was actually mine. What I would choose to do with it was now the question. Firstly I took personal ownership and responsibility for everything that had happened in my adult years and set about making changes in the areas I did not like. Slowly, one by one, I made better choices, which in turn began to produce better results. Remember good things take time.

It was phenomenal, yet very basic. I had to make some hard calls which some people close to me didn't like but I was never more clear about what I had to do to begin to CHOOSE A GREAT LIFE. Please don't skip over this topic going "yeah, yeah". Take the time to get this locked into your belief system. If you do, it will change how you CHOOSE to take responsibility for your life.

I can now honestly say with my hand on my heart "I love my Life!!" – this life I love so much was created by making solid, well informed choices and decisions and also having good support systems and people around me.

This doesn't mean I don't make mistakes – I still do, but I make many more right choices than wrong ones now, so it keeps me moving in the right direction. Life really does get better and better in so many ways.

You can do this – start today, change begins now. It's a matter of Choice.

The power and opportunity of choice are always available to us. That is very exciting.

"One of the greatest feelings in life is the conviction that you have lived the life you wanted to live – with the rough and the smooth, the good and the bad – but yours, shaped by your own choices, and not someone else's." **MICHAEL IGNATIEFF**[3]

Heather says
"It's All About Choice"

Girltalk Challenge

I urge you to take the next few days to consider carefully the 'Power of Choice'. Begin to think about the next series of choices you are going to make in your journey of living a Great Life.

Remember it's your life and the choices you make about how you want to live it should be yours. If you value your life and you want to live a Great Life, then, please, take the time to fully understand it is all in the choices you make from this point on.

The concept of excellence

Every one of us has the ability to achieve something greater than we imagine. Every one of us has excellence within us – not just some of us, EVERY ONE OF US. Every person has a seed of excellence in some area of her or his life and it has the potential to produce something entirely different, but equally brilliant. We are all called to achieve something different but equally significant, which is why it's unhelpful to compare yourself with others.

We are not born to be average; each one of us has a unique talent with the ability to be excellent in that area. Whether we choose to be excellent or not is our own decision. Remember the slogan "If it's to be, it's up to me". Living a life less than this is a life not yet fully realised. A life of excellence is a journey, but a journey definitely worth taking. Cultivate excellence within you so it continues to expand and grow, taking you on a journey to new heights.

Excellence is achievable for every one of us and excellence brings a great sense of accomplishment. Having the desire to put the extra effort into everything we do is something we must cultivate. For most of us it probably doesn't come naturally, but if you desire to be excellent you can develop this into natural behaviour until it becomes an instinctive way of thinking and doing. Then you will get to a place where you do not settle for anything less and your eye and attitude are on excellence every time.

Excellence is not perfection, but being the very best you can be, putting your very best into everything you do and knowing you have done everything you know to achieve the best possible outcome. This is an excellent effort. Extra effort will always bring a more excellent result.

Once you begin to experience it, you will not want to settle for less. Once you have experienced something great, 'good' is not good enough any more. In fact, just 'good' or 'okay' will annoy you because you will recognise the unrealised potential and you will not be able to help yourself lift good to great, which will then be excellent! Then you will experience a place of Greater Reward.

When you are determined to be excellent and prepared to do the extra that excellence requires, you begin to realise excellence does give you a greater reward in the areas of your life where you are applying it. Greater satisfaction, greater excitement, greater financial gain, greater joy, greater fun, greater pleasure, greater contentment and so on because there is a wonderful feeling that goes with bringing your best forward and doing the very best you can.

Don't settle for less; 'average' isn't good enough for any one of us. Please don't choose average. You are capable of much more. So be a 'Woman of Excellence' and make a difference to your own life and the lives of those around you. Enjoy the rewards you will earn along the way when you step into excellence.

Luck just doesn't happen to us; we make it and excellence in everything we do will bring a lot of 'luck'. Someone once said "the harder I work, the luckier I get". What we sow we will eventually reap. It's a natural law of life none of us can escape. Sowing seeds of excellence and reaping an excellent harvest in the area we planted go hand in hand. It's an exciting truth!

Taste and experience a greater reward; it is sweet, smooth and delicious, and worth every bit of extra effort. When looking at and thinking about the word and the meaning of excellence, we might be tempted to feel it's not achievable, but excellence is achieved step by step in the little things and in the detail of everyday life.

If we really want to become a 'Woman of Excellence' and we want to be moving towards excellence in all areas of our life, we must accept continuous improvement is required. Excellence doesn't necessarily make demands on you but, when embraced with a positive attitude, it gives us an opportunity to expand ourselves.

Excellence is not something attained by merely just wanting it, or waiting for it to come to you, it must be pursued. It must be a heartfelt thing coming from deep within you, a desire to do something that shines.

If we are not moving forward and upward in our daily walk, we are either standing still or sliding backwards, so it is important we are moving forward even it if is step by step, day by day. Small steps will take you a long way. It's a process and a journey which can be exciting and fun.

Regardless of where we are at in our lives and what's going on, we can begin this journey at any time we decide; it's our choice. The decision is ours and ours alone. We can begin at any moment and each new moment offers another opportunity to choose a higher path - The Path of Excellence.

Please understand excellence is not perfection. Striving for perfection will bring you much frustration and disappointment because it's not often achievable but excellence most certainly is. Remember, when you bring your very best forward it will be excellent.

When the decision is made in our hearts and minds to choose to be excellent, we begin our journey to higher ground. In order for this to happen, we need to be completely honest with ourselves about areas of our lives which are not working as well as we would like them to be. I believe we all have areas requiring attention.

Sometimes we ignore these areas because we don't know how to deal with them or we see them as too difficult for now - so we tell ourselves they are not really a problem - but choosing excellence means these areas need your attention.

We need to be willing to get out of our comfort zone and out of our places of habit and take a good look. This takes a willing attitude and a determined decision. We need to ask ourselves how badly we want something better for our life and whether we are prepared to do whatever it takes!

DEFINITION:

Excellence[4] - Possessing outstanding quality or superior merit; remarkably good. The quality of excelling; possessing good qualities in high degree; an outstanding feature.

If we want something better for our lives we will have to do something different. Just wishing will not make it happen; it takes action.

Excellence is something to be pursued and sought after; it doesn't just happen along the way! Take your natural abilities and God-given talents and do your very best with them - not compromising or being complacent with opportunities and responsibilities. Much of how we live our life is done out of habit, not necessarily by making conscious decisions. It's important to identify areas of habit and reassess them. Once identified, habits can be broken. Identifying them is often the challenge. It takes focus and honesty.

We have to CHOOSE to be Excellent. It's a decision and there are sacrifices that go with that decision. Are you willing to make that sacrifice?? That in itself is the first choice.

What have we done to excellence? It's been downgraded to average. Make sure you really understand at what level excellence occurs; excellence is so much more than average or mediocre. Average appears to have taken the place of excellent in many areas of our lives. It's our choice whether we continue to accept this. Society has downgraded excellent to average.

There used to be a time when excellence or being extraordinary was something we all aspired to. Now it can be a problem for people reaching out for excellence to get support from those around them. Don't be afraid to stand alone if you have to or seek out those who think the same as you and stay close to these people.

Not everyone you have contact with will support your changes. Being excellent often makes others feel uncomfortable. When making changes for yourself it may have a ripple effect on others around you. Stay focused and determined. Believe in yourself and know what you believe in is the right way for you. Self belief is the key to staying on track when others distract you.

Excellence - Crave it, Pursue it, and Go After it!

- Make excellence a lifestyle choice and walk in continuous improvement of yourself and your life.
- Do not strive for perfection, but rather choose excellence over average in all you do and you will experience the reward which goes with the decision to choose a life of excellence.
- Commit to doing more than required in every situation. This is how excellence is established. Excellence often comes out of the EXTRA.
- Foster the Spirit of Excellence and do not be discouraged by others who do not make the same choices.
- Do not be discouraged by those who criticise, mock and undermine excellence.

Excellence does become an art form which causes the eye, mind and spirit to clearly see a better way in all things and proceeds to achieve it. When you seek and apply excellence, your true potential begins to rise within you.

Understand the ART OF EXCELLENCE and MAKE IT A LIFESTYLE.

66

Personal Comment:

Excellence is indeed a beautiful thing and most people instantly recognise a Spirit of Excellence at work. I personally have found a lot of obstacles in my journey of achieving excellence. I have discovered and been surprised at how many people object to excellence. I believe it's because they may at times feel threatened by it – I encourage you not to be put off by that!

On your journey of excellence, be careful not to compare yourself with others; this is your personal journey of being the best you can be. That in itself is excellence. This particular topic is a favourite of mine, as I have worked hard - and continue to work hard - to maintain excellence in all I do. I don't always achieve it, depending on time and priority; however, I am always working towards it.

I believe that in itself displays an excellent attitude. There will be times when you may have to choose to do 'less' rather than spread yourself too thinly. When you are over-extended with your time, excellence can be difficult to achieve. You may then feel disappointed, but I have learnt to do a little less and do it the best I can to feel satisfied and happy with the result.

At times, things happen out of my control to compromise excellence, but I have learnt not to sweat the small stuff. I choose what to let go and what to be persistent with, to keep the big picture in view. Don't be too hard on yourself if something falls below your expectation – change what you can, then move on. Tomorrow is another day with another opportunity.

Pursuing excellence has helped bring out my gifts and talents and put them to good use. This has expanded me enormously as a person, and actually I have surprised myself on many occasions to find what I have stored up inside waiting to be released. When you give excellence the time and opportunity to be exposed, you will be amazed at how creative you are.

I was once told the majority of people are content to just do the bare essentials in life and no more, just enough to get by. I think this is quite sad because so much potential is then lost. I see evidence around me of this appearing to be true...but deep down inside of me I believe everyone wants to be excellent or really outstanding at something (and they can be). Maybe they just need encouragement or someone to believe in them, but let's start with ourselves and be an excellent example to those around us.

The Spirit of Excellence can be contagious when displayed with humility.

Heather says
"A Life of excellence is a life worth living"

Girltalk Challenge

Consider something you have done recently, go back to it and add the extra excellence factor to it. See the difference you can make. You will be delighted at the result.

Start with just a couple of little things and the spirit of excellence will begin to get stirred up in you. Have fun doing it!

Your time is your life

Time is your Most Valuable Asset. Planning how you use it is one of the most important things you can do.

Our life is a time span of approximately 81 years for women;
0 – 10 – 20 – 30 – 40 – 50 – 60 – 70 – 75 – 80 – 85 – where are you on the line? Have you begun to live the life you have always wanted? If not, it's time to start. It's never too late to begin.

I have just begun to realise the importance of almost every moment. This is my life, my one chance to do something significant, something that will stay, long after I am gone. I don't want to waste a moment more. I am in the second half of my life and I want to finish well. The moments go so fast – the moments into hours, the hours into days, days into weeks, weeks into months, months into years. There is my life. There goes my life!

I am still learning to manage and prioritise my time more effectively. It is an ongoing challenge. Women have a tendency to cram too much into their day. It's time to get ruthless and toss away a few things. Ask yourself how absolutely necessary is everything you do? Would your world collapse if you removed and stopped doing 30% of it? I don't think so.

We are often deceived into thinking everything we do is essential when it's not at all. Sometimes it's just a terrible habit of filling every space in the day with something. When we do this we miss the things that are important to us. Being busy will rob you of the enjoyment of what you do and, more importantly, rob you of your REAL LIFE. It is important not to give your time away; do not allow others to steal your time, so you do not have the time to do the things important to you.

Don't waste your time. It's important to have a base plan to work to; if you don't, your precious time will be eaten away. Remember TIME IS ACTUALLY YOUR LIFE. If we don't get enough time to do the things important to us we get resentful and bad tempered and begin to blame others for our own dissatisfaction. It's your life – choose to spend it wisely. Think of your time as your money – you SPEND IT. How are you spending your life? Once it's spent, you don't get it back.

Take a look at how you are spending your time. Delete things that are not important or productive. Be honest with yourself about time-wasters e.g. watching television, surfing the internet, unnecessary shopping, unnecessary and extended conversations.

Identify areas which are not adding anything productive or positive to your life and remove them from your day to allow something enjoyable into its space. There are certain things in our lives we must do in order to function correctly. However, sometimes we end up doing things that put pressure on ourselves and are not useful or helpful to anyone.

Women often sacrifice themselves too much, leaving nothing for their own wellbeing and in turn lose their joy in life. We need to allocate time for ourselves to help us function wholly and happily.

Don't put too much in your day. This creates pressure so you cannot enjoy what you are doing. Cramming doesn't necessarily achieve more in the long run; sort out priorities and do these well and you will enjoy your day so much more, and you may be surprised how much better you perform.

You don't want to get to the end of your life and have never done the things you really wanted to do. Certainly we have responsibilities, but often women give away time specifically meant for their own wellbeing. We do have responsibilities to ourselves as well as others; don't rob yourself, particularly of creative things which make you feel alive and bring peace and healing to your soul.

Check your balance of time and get your priorities sorted out. You will be surprised how much time you have and what you can achieve comfortably, and still have time for fun. Balance in all things is the key to success in your life. As a woman you have a lot of things in your life and you have an enormous capacity for achievement. However, we need to realise that without a well managed balance in each area, longevity can not be sustained.

Women are great jugglers and at times have to juggle a lot of balls, but to keep all the balls in the air, one ball cannot be much bigger or heavier than the rest. When that happens, juggling becomes more difficult.

Keep the balls balanced. Assess each area of your life regularly to check whether any area needs more attention or whether one area is getting too much attention at the expense of others. We instinctively know when this happens and should rectify it quickly before it causes a problem. We hear the word 'balance' a lot these days, but it is the key to a happy life for you and others close to you.

Relaxation, exercise and recreation are a must to help keep work and family focus a joy. As women we need to realise it is not selfish to take care of our own needs.

Be confident about choosing how you want to spend your time. Not in a selfish way but in a way that is wise and considers all of what is important to you. Balance your time well.

A guideline might be:

24 hours in a day:
- 8 hours sleep/rest
- 8 hours work
- 1 hour exercise
- 2 hours nourishment/meals
- 5 hours family/recreation

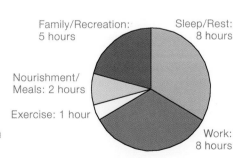

Family/Recreation: 5 hours

Sleep/Rest: 8 hours

Nourishment/Meals: 2 hours

Exercise: 1 hour

Work: 8 hours

Obviously this will be different for each woman's situation so is only a guideline or suggestion to help you check how and where you are spending your time.

Maybe your graph will look different but doing the exercise will help you identify how you are spending your time and what changes you may wish to make.

- Live your life well. Your time and your life are one and the same.
- Plan your time. Prioritise and manage it.
- Don't let unnecessary things rob your time away from you.
- Balance your time with things important to you (be ruthless).
- Take moments of time whenever and wherever you can; capture time and space. There is much pleasure in that. A moment to be still and reflect on the good things is a lovely thing to do for yourself.
- Time can be your enemy or your friend. Choose to make it your friend.
- Make time a priority for yourself and it will nurture you, and heal you, in many ways.
- Allow time to be kind to you.
- It's better to give fewer things more of your time, than more things less – quality not quantity.
- Be smart and strategic with your time. Time has a great value – it's YOUR LIFE!
- Allow yourself to experience many moments of time and space. There is beauty in time alone, with no other attachments.
- Time is a beautiful thing. Enjoy yours.
- Live a great life with the time allocated to you and your purpose.

Personal Comment:

I recently heard Joyce Meyer say we need to build 'Margin' into our day, so we have time to enjoy.

This is my year of doing just that. Eliminating things which don't bring me joy or just waste my time and energy - giving myself this time to enjoy my life, because my time is my life.

I recently heard a very successful businessman say we need to apply the 80/20 rule to our time and life. His view was 80% of what we do is not productive, or of little value. We need to spend more time on the 20% that matters to us, brings the most joy and produces the most results.

Because I am in the second half of my life I now frequently remind myself I do not want to get to the end of my days and not have done all that was important to me. So now I plan the things that are important to me and I am making sure these things get done! When I reach my final days, more than anything I want to be pleased with how I spent my life. I want the same for YOU! Let's have no regrets.

As women, we really need to start to 'get this'.

HEATHER SAYS
"YOUR TIME IS YOUR LIFE - SPEND IT WISELY"

GIRLTALK CHALLENGE

Draw yourself a time graph and make the adjustments
where necessary.

By just spending time on your graph and being honest with
yourself you will quickly identify what needs changing.

Do it for your family too – it's a great thing to do together -
so your family members know they are important to you and
they have an important place in your graph.

The power of the written word

It is important to understand the power of writing down your visions, dreams and goals. Your written vision (or plan) is your road map to take you to your destination. If you want to go to a place you have never been before, you will take the best and shortest route if you follow your map (written plan).

I know there is power in the written word and I believe in it. The more detailed the goal is written, the stronger it becomes and the clearer the focus. Having goals broken down into small bite-sized pieces makes them more easily digestible and more fulfilling, as you achieve little steps along the way.

I must tell you most of what I have achieved and some of the most amazing things that have happened for me have been part of a written plan. Now, not all was part of a written plan; I have had some wonderful unexpected surprises along the way, which have been icing on the cake.

Be an avid writer of your goals and your success rate of seeing these goals come to fruition will be very high indeed! It has been proven that people who have their goals written down have a high success rate of achieving them, compared to those who don't.

It is very important to:

- Take the time to clearly establish your goals and what you truly want from each area of your life.
- Write each goal in a specific and detailed manner – then place a realistic time frame on it.
- Keep the document on hand to read regularly. This will keep you on track!
- Identify distractions and other situations which 'pop up' to take you off course. Eliminate those things immediately, understanding they are not part of your plan. (Unless, of course, you choose to make them so.)
- Being a little flexible is good, but not so much that you begin to alter your course, unless it adds value to your goal.

All your decision-making will then become easier because, unless what is happening lines up with your goal, it will be eliminated or put aside for another time. This will help you narrow your focus to all things relating to your goal, increasing your chance of succeeding without wasting time, energy and finance.

I believe God does honour clarity of mind, planning, organisation and a grateful and positive attitude.

Don't delay, write your goals today!

PERSONAL COMMENT:

For many years every January, I have taken the time to identify and focus on what I want to achieve in the year ahead. To help me do this, I separate the different areas of my life: marriage, family, relationships, friendships, health/exercise, professional/career, finances, leisure/creativity and other. I write down under each heading my goal or my desire for that area of my life.

I check what I have written frequently to make sure I am on track, making the necessary adjustments promptly and ensuring the goal is still appropriate and desirable. I also have to make some choices about the things I need to let go of to make way for new and exciting things I want to do in the year ahead.

This helps me clarify and stay focused with my decision-making throughout the year. I sometimes add extra little things in along the way, to add unexpected fun and variety.

Keep your goals realistic and achieve them one by one, celebrating each achievement as you go. It's a lot of fun writing and fulfilling short term and long term goals. If you don't know where to start, just start with something very small which can be achieved quickly and go from there. As you do this, you can then move to bigger and more exciting things.

Although it is good to keep goals realistic I also like to have a separate list of goals which are unrealistically wild. This helps me not limit myself to just what I know I can do. It is also helpful in stretching myself to think above and beyond my own ability.

You will be amazed at how you begin to move towards that which you have committed to paper.

GIRLTALK CHALLENGE

Dear Girlfriend,

If you have not written down your goals, your desires and your dreams, I urge you to do it now.

Start with small, short term ones, for each important area of your life; then move on to more long term ones. By short term I mean within a week or month; then move it to half yearly and yearly.

In the discipline of writing, it will help you identify what's in your heart.

Don't delay – do it today!

Advice from experienced counsel

We all know we are not experts in everything – there are times when advice is required from those more experienced than we are in certain matters.

- Do not be afraid to put your hand up and say "HELP!" Asking for help is not admitting failure, it's a sign of being courageous and smart. Seek the correct advice from the appropriate place. This is not a defeat; it is taking control in an intelligent way.
- Do not stay in a place of inaction when you become stuck.
- Do not let pride stand in your way of overcoming a problem.

Many women wait too long before asking for help (some never ask for help at all). If you have had several attempts at solving your problem and it has not worked out for you, it's time to seek help.

- Be determined and willing to do whatever it takes to succeed and to work things out in a positive and productive way.
- Be careful to seek advice from people qualified and experienced in the area of your problem and from people who have their own life together.
- Check out the credentials of the person you are seeking advice from.
- Don't rush around telling all your friends and work colleagues your problem. Choose carefully who you seek advice from – you don't want everyone gossiping about your personal business.
- Girlfriends are usually not experienced, qualified or impartial enough to give you good advice on important matters.

Personal Comment:

Seek experienced counsel with a specialist in the area of your concern. I regularly get outside advice from people more experienced than I am in certain areas. However, I will still make my own decision once I am well informed. Often the advice I get clarifies the decision I want to make. So it is smart to ask for help or advice – just don't leave it too long, or let your situation get out of hand before seeking experienced advice!

I have discovered there is a solution to most problems, if you just ask the right people. Try not to let your pride get in the way. I have seen many of my friends go through some unnecessary things because they are too prideful to ask for help. I don't believe we are designed to do things alone; in fact, quite the opposite.

Sometimes we women can be too independent, because we are very capable and asking for help can be difficult. But believe when you do, you usually wish you had done it sooner.

"Two are better than one because they have a good reward for their labour." ECCLESIASTES 4:9[6]

"...a three fold cord is not quickly broken."
ECCLESIASTES 4:12[6]

Heather says
"Asking for help is being a smart girl"

GIRLTALK CHALLENGE

Is there something you have been struggling with lately? Perhaps you just can't find the answer or are unsure of what to do?

Find someone credible who may be able to help you and go ask for help. If they can't help you, they may know someone who can.

Don't struggle with a situation alone. Share your burden; often a problem shared is a problem solved.

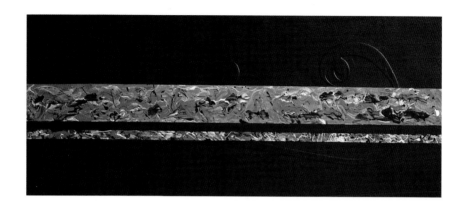

BE STRONG
Find the strength within you

Walk in integrity

It is essential to have a set of values or standards firmly planted in your belief system to define who you are. It is important to try not to go below these standards.

These are your foundation or platform by which you live. This is the foundation to guide and hold you in the right place when you are shaken, or when something comes your way to shake your beliefs.

- Try not to compromise your values – they are an expression of your character and personality that defines you. These values define you and are the foundation of your reputation. These are the things people think of when they think of you. Hold these values firmly in place.
- When you allow your values to be compromised, the fabric of who you are will begin to break down and you will feel discouraged and disillusioned with yourself.
- Don't sell yourself out to please others. Stick firmly to what you believe in, because at the end of the day you will be responsible for your own decisions and actions.
- Don't lower your standard because others won't raise theirs. Sometimes you will have to stand alone.
- True integrity often stands alone.

DEFINITION:

Integrity[7] - Honesty, honour, incorruptibility, principles, righteousness, uprightness, soundness.

There are sacrifices to be made to walk in integrity and you will need to be prepared to make them. Not everyone will feel comfortable with you when you make a decision based on integrity. Some relationships may come under pressure; be prepared for this, but do not be swayed into compromising what is important to you. If you do, you will not be happy with yourself.

- You will walk strongly and confidently in integrity, when you have firmly established your values, having a strong sense of moral ethics and justice.
- When you walk in integrity you always do the right thing regardless of the circumstance and who is involved. You will be consistent and people will know they can rely on you.

Living a life of integrity will earn you respect from others, in particular from the people who are most important to you. Walking in integrity keeps your conscience clear and you will be at peace with yourself. Pursue integrity and live by it, even when you are alone with yourself. What you do when you are alone will determine what you do in public.

Integrity does not just show itself in front of others. True integrity is established firmly in your core being and is at work all the time outwardly and inwardly.

PERSONAL COMMENT:

I have had to stand alone many times, to hold firmly to what I believe in. Others have sometimes been challenged by my refusal to compromise myself. It has been very difficult, but I can hold my head up knowing I haven't sold my soul. Everybody may not like me, but I like myself for sticking to my values. I have discovered integrity will usually show itself at the end of the day. Don't be a person who agrees with everyone, or anything. Stand firmly in your own beliefs and values.

Integrity is very important to me. I know I am not perfect but my intention to do the right thing at all times is firmly in place. Keeping my intentions pure is important to me and I try not to act until I know my intentions are in the right place.

I make mistakes at times (as we all do) but integrity also means admitting your mistakes quickly and apologising. This will hold your reputation in place if you slip up. Having integrity helps me to sleep well and peacefully. Integrity is a choice to be made ahead of time, because situations do arise at times that will catch you off guard unless you are walking in integrity in all you do.

HEATHER SAYS
"WALK IN HAND IN HAND WITH INTEGRITY"

GIRLTALK CHALLENGE

Establish a set of values important enough to you for you to feel comfortable standing strong in and which you can enhance your reputation on.

For example:
> I will stay true to my word at all times.
> I will speak out when I know injustice has taken place.
> I will consider carefully the needs of others.
> I will stand firm for the things I believe in.

An honest contribution in the workplace

To make an honest contribution, you must have a good work ethic and a good attitude. You need to believe in what you are doing and who you are doing it for, eliminating personal agenda and negative opinion. Always work in the best interest of the company and the people you work for. Keep the 'Greater Purpose' to the forefront of what you do. Every employment position offers opportunity for you to shine if you choose to see it that way.

Choosing a job in line with your natural talent and God-given gifts will help to achieve fulfilment and success. Do what you do with passion to keep your work exciting and rewarding.

Have a serving/giving attitude with the aim of helping others around you and not only working for yourself. This shows exceptional character. Have the ability to understand it's not about you - the output of the team is always greater than the output of the individual. Extend a helping hand to those around you. Service before self will get you noticed.

Set an example over and above the normal standard in the workplace. Recognise what the 'normal standard' is; deliberately go about raising your standard above this level and help others to raise their standard along with you. Be careful to do this in a positive and encouraging way.

Going the extra mile when no one else does is admirable and will be recognised and rewarded at the right time. Going the extra mile is a mark of excellence, but don't just expect to do it once; it needs to be a consistent part of your expectation of yourself. Extra should be your norm.

Value and respect your employer and work colleagues – this is a superior and attractive quality. An employer recognises respect from employees – be a person your boss wants to work with.

These attributes are very powerful and bring great reward to personal and professional lives. Nothing beats being the 'best' you can be. Making an honest contribution in the workplace will gain you the promotion you are seeking. Good things do come to those whose attitude is right and to those who wait patiently and diligently.

An honest contribution is one where you willingly and cheerfully give your best. Giving your best at all times, not just some of the time, is an honest contribution. Bringing all that you have to offer is an honest contribution.

Other attributes of an honest contribution are:

- Being early to work, without claiming or expecting payment for it
- Staying later to complete a task well and with excellence
- Going the extra mile, knowing it will bring a better result
- Working harder and faster whenever possible, especially when a critical deadline looms
- Bringing a bright and cheery disposition to the environment you work in
- Extending a hand to others
- Not taking short cuts, doing the task correctly
- Valuing and respecting the company you work for
- Valuing and respecting your employer as a person
- Wanting your company to succeed and understanding your contribution to that success. (This is very valuable to your employer.)
- Service above self will always bring greater reward.

Most of us spend the majority of our lives in the workplace, so it's important we take personal responsibility for making it a happy and rewarding place to be. As an employee, you are the one with the power to set the mood and atmosphere in your place of employment. Learn to love your job by developing a positive attitude and recognising the difference you can make.

Ask yourself: "Am I truly engaged in my work or am I just going through the motions?" If you are not 'engaged', improve or remove yourself. You are of little value to yourself or others in a workplace where you are not prepared to be and give your best. You will also be an obstacle to others wanting to do their best.

66

Personal Comment:

When we consistently bring our best and make an honest contribution to our place of work, I believe there will be a reward. What you sow, you will eventually reap. Many people get impatient and expect instant reward without an honest contribution. I am experiencing this more and more often from people who don't know what an honest contribution is – they have never been taught or even seen a good example of it.

As an employer, I can recognise very quickly those who are bringing an honest contribution, those who are 'fully engaged' in their work and those who are just going through the motions doing the minimum.

People who are 'fully engaged' in their work are more knowledgeable in their field, because they are attentive. They understand and embrace their responsibilities and the difference they make to the results. Their hearts are in their work; they show confidence because they know they are valued; because they know they are bringing an honest contribution they have nothing to hide.

The people I like on my team are those who can look you in the eye when communicating, are happy, comfortable asking questions and admitting their mistakes. I love working with these people; they have their values in a healthy place. They can be trusted. The people who bring an honest contribution are easily recognisable and are the people I think of first when I am in a position to promote or reward.

HEATHER SAYS
"PEOPLE WHO MAKE AN HONEST CONTRIBUTION
ARE A PLEASURE TO HAVE ON THE TEAM"

99

GIRLTALK CHALLENGE

Make a list of the things you know you can do better in your place of work. List ways to help your boss and your work colleagues. Start doing these one by one.

Think of ways you can make your work environment a happier place. You could be the one who leads the way for others. You could be the one in line for the next promotion. Be a leader, not a follower.

Check your intention – keep your motives pure and honest. Don't underestimate your employer or boss's ability to really see what is going on.

Sowing and reaping

I believe every thought, word and action we partake in plants a seed which will eventually bring us a harvest; good, bad or otherwise. It's part of the law of sowing and reaping which none of us can avoid. What you give out comes back to you.

It is very important to keep your thoughts positive, productive and passionate and to always have a spirit of goodwill toward ourselves and to others. The seeds we plant are powerful tools in determining the outcome of the harvest in our lives.

Our actions speak volumes about who we really are and what we are made of. If we consider our thoughts, words and actions as seeds, then before planting we can consider carefully the type of harvest we want in our future. Every moment of every day, the choice is ours. Many of us know and believe this, but somehow in everyday life we forget it.

"So in everything do to others what you would have them do to you." MATTHEW 7:12⁸

I have discovered "What you sow, you will eventually reap" to be one of the most important lessons in life: What am I thinking? What am I speaking? What am I doing? I believe that it's that simple; check it out, test yourself!

"A man reaps what he sows." GALATIANS 6:7⁸

PERSONAL COMMENT:

I have learnt this one, big time. In fact it makes me so nervous I try never to forget it, keeping it in the forefront of all I do.

I believe no-one escapes the "what you sow, you reap" principle. On a positive note, you have an opportunity to create an abundant harvest for yourself and others by sowing beautiful seed everywhere you go.

Good seed, fertile seed, healthy seed = Abundant Harvest. Consider the opposite.

No good deed ever escapes a payback on some level - not that I do good deeds purely for payback, not at all; actually it never enters my mind. Helping others is a strong natural instinct in me, I just have to do it! However, it never ceases to amaze me that somewhere, somehow I almost always receive a blessing in return. It surprises me every time.

As I get older it is one of my greatest desires to sow beautiful seeds everywhere I go – seeds full of colour and fragrance.

HEATHER SAYS
"PLANT YOURSELF A BEAUTIFUL GARDEN"

GIRLTALK CHALLENGE

Take a bagful of beautiful seeds with you each day and plant as you go. Watch as the law of sowing and reaping begins to bring a beautiful harvest to your life.

Begin today to plant a beautiful garden. Start with your thoughts, words and deeds. It will not fail you.

Conquering fear

Fear can be a very debilitating thing. Most of us experience this on a regular basis, even in little ways we don't always recognise, so it is important to recognise it, understand it and take control of it – so it does not control you and your decisions for your life.

Fear keeps you in a place of limitation, it keeps you from growing, moving forward and progressing in your life.

- Operating out of fear holds you back from your destiny. It steals what is rightfully yours in your life.
- Don't let fear stop you from reaching out and moving forward.
- Do not make decisions based on fear and negative emotion. Inform yourself and take control of the situation you find yourself in; make firm and decisive decisions based on fact. Do not let fearful emotions and negative thinking run your mind. This can be quite paralysing and hold you in a place of inaction.
- Apply the positive thinking theory. Delete negative thinking and replace with positive affirmation.
- Fear keeps you from making the right decisions for yourself and others you are responsible for.
- Deal firmly with your fear to ensure your decision-making is well balanced. Caution is helpful, fear is not.
- The perception of something is very different to the reality. Break it down so you can identify what is real and what is not.

Some things we most fear:

- Fear of failure
- Fear of rejection
- Fear of losing something or someone
- Fear of criticism
- Fear of change
- Fear of lack of money or provision

- Fear of how much we will have to sacrifice or give up
- Fear of being out of God's Will.

Recognise fear for what it is by recalling the well-known acronym "FEAR = False Evidence Appearing Real". Conquer it with faith, positive thought and affirmation. Arm yourself with the facts of the situation and most often the thing you fear most will never happen. When those waves of fear come, do not give in to them; fear is an emotion with no basis other than negative thought.

Faith is the opposite of Fear – having faith and belief about your life and what you are capable of achieving is important to overcome fear. Keep your thinking positive and full of affirmation. When you build your life on faith, facts and wisdom, you live life more freely and effectively and you certainly have more fun.

Personal Comment:

In the past I had a lot of trouble with fear. It controlled me and stole my joy in situations which should have been happy for me.

I now have a strategy for when fear comes near:

- Remove emotion
- Focus on the facts
- Develop a plan
- Prepare well
- Execute with confidence

I recently had an experience which put my overcoming fear theory to the test yet again. (It is definitely an ongoing challenge.) No sooner do you conquer one thing, another pops up, but that is all part of this wonderful life we live. Hopefully we get stronger and more confident as we go.

My husband purchased me a bungy jump from the Kawarau Bridge in Queenstown, New Zealand. We have been holidaying in Queenstown for 15 years and on each visit I would think about bungy jumping but never had the courage to do it. My imagination would think of all the things that could go wrong; fear would overcome me and I would become paralysed just thinking about it.

This year, I made the decision I would not come home from my Queenstown holiday again without doing the bungy jump. So I planned a strategy to overcome my fear of the dreaded bungy jump:

- Put a time frame on the event (e.g. before a certain date).
- Booked the jump for the first appointment of the day, so I didn't have to wait in queue and get even more nervous and fearful while waiting.
- Told the young man putting my harness on and tying my legs together I did not want a long countdown, only 3...2...1...GO and told him to say it really quickly.
- Made the decision to close my eyes and definitely not look down.
- Did not allow my mind to wander.
- Recited facts I knew about the bungy, e.g. no-one has ever had an accident bungying from the Kawarau Bridge in Queenstown, New Zealand; I am more likely to have a car accident; most people want to do it again because they love it so much and so on.
- Determined in my heart and mind I would do this and overcome the nagging fear of this activity, and then holiday in Queenstown in peace.
- Told myself 'God has not given me a spirit of fear, but of power, love and sound mind'.

"It is helpful to remind ourselves
that Fear does not come from a sound mind" 2 TIMOTHY 1:7 [6]

I went through with it and am thrilled I did. It was not as bad as I thought, though there was one moment when I felt the fear rush through me - the split second before I left the platform. It was at this moment I had the choice of giving in to fear or pushing through. I pushed through it and DIVED out into space.

What did I learn?

- Identify exactly what it is that you fear, take a good look at it, face it down and speak to it.
- Plan a strategy to put you in control of the situation.
- Calculate the risk based on facts not emotions.
- Some of the best things in life lie beyond the fear barrier.

That bungy jump redefined my perception of fear and I understand more clearly than ever before that fear is not reality. Since doing the bungy jump, I feel more confident in my ability to overcome fear. I also have a greater sense of my ability to achieve all I desire if I approach things based on balanced information and facts.

You certainly don't have to do a bungy jump or anything like it, you just need to identify one thing you fear and develop a plan to overcome it. Start with something small to gain your confidence, then work up to the bigger things holding you back from your potential.

For me, the bungy jump was a catalyst in redefining fear in my own life and releasing a new level of potential. Fear no longer controls me, and I must say girls, it's very liberating! I am astonished to realise how much fear controlled my life in the past. The best is certainly yet to come, now I have learnt not to give in to fear.

Fear is such a dream killer, don't let it rob you! Take charge of it and begin to live as you know you should.

I have discovered the stronger my faith gets the weaker fear is in my life. I regularly check my Faith and Fear scale. By keeping my faith strong, I keep fear at a distance. Conquering fear and keeping it powerless in my life is a continual battle, but one that can be won through faith - faith in God, faith in myself, faith in my family.

HEATHER SAYS
"FAITH WILL HELP YOU CONQUER FEAR"

GIRLTALK CHALLENGE

Think of one small thing you are fearful of and isolate it, look at it front on and speak to it.

For example – "I will not let you control me any longer"

Develop a plan of how you will overcome it based on facts, not on emotion. Keep anger and hurt out of the plan.

Put a date and time on when you are going to do it. Gather support from family and friends to help you. Believe you deserve to be full of confidence, courage and faith.

Once you have done this, something inside you will change and I believe you will begin to realise fear is not the truth. I can assure you when you approach things with a plan based on facts, the thing you fear is not nearly as difficult as you thought. You will realise it did not deserve the anxiety it caused you.

I believe you can do it, because I have been there.

Good always outweighs bad

Most situations can be turned into something positive if the right attitude and effort is applied to it. I am not talking about extreme or exceptional circumstances, but to life in general. Of course, I am aware there are some much more complex situations. However, I believe the above is true of everyday life.

Your attitude is paramount. Keep a positive and caring attitude at all times. This will help you overcome most things – the mind is a powerful tool to control and manage situations. This is in line with positive thinking. Keep your heart attitude in line with a positive mind.

> "For as he thinks in his heart, so is he" **PROVERBS 23:7**⁶

Think about the good outcome you want, and begin to walk towards it, doing what is necessary to overcome. At any time, a negative situation can be turned into a positive one with the right attitude, words and action. It may take some time, but keep doing it and I believe it will work. Good will prevail.

Imparting something good into a less than desirable situation will move the situation in the right direction. There is hope in all situations when you apply goodness, kindness, love and understanding.

Being part of imparting good everywhere you go can be most exhilarating. To be able to watch situations change before your eyes helps you understand what we are really here for and what we can do with the opportunities before us. There is power in imparting something good (positive) into a bad (negative) situation. Life is about imparting something good into people's lives and circumstances every day, so bring a blessing and leave a blessing wherever you go – good thoughts, good intentions, good words, good deeds.

Yes, there are terrible things that happen in the world, but there are many more wonderful things going on. Let's focus on those things. When we do this, it brings about more good things. Be willing participants in doing good. If we participate in only that which is good, loving, kind, forgiving and understanding, good will outweigh bad in our own life and the lives of those around us.

Personal Comment:

Love may not necessarily conquer all instantly, but I have discovered putting something loving and kind into difficult and unpleasant situations begins to improve them. Keep doing this for long enough and you will see a bad situation turn around. The key here is don't give up. It does take time in most cases but it will happen!

I personally have waited a long time for some things to change and I can tell you, if you don't give up you will see good emerge. I have many examples of this in my own life. This principle is the truth.

Although at times it is difficult to keep on imparting something positive when you don't physically see any change, I choose to believe good will prevail. Decide how committed you are to seeing a positive change. As Sir Winston Churchill said "Never, never, never give up."

I have had a situation in my life where I continued to put something loving and kind into a very hurtful situation for almost two years. I found it difficult to do this and mostly didn't feel like doing it, but made an unemotional decision to do it regardless of how I felt.

The situation went from looking like no hope at all, to a major turnaround after two years. The turnaround came through my persistence. During the two years, I kept believing good would conquer evil. I kept telling myself it had to, because it is part of my faith and I would not doubt it.

I am very happy to report the situation is very different today – there has been reconciliation and peace between both parties. I recognise the lesson for me was to pursue peace wherever possible. I realise it will not always be achievable because other people have free will too, but even then peace would come through my knowing I had imparted something good from my end.

HEATHER SAYS
"THE GOOD IN YOU WILL WIN, SO DEVELOP
THE GOOD IN YOU"

"If we live good lives, the times are also good.
As we are, such are the times." ST AUGUSTINE⁹

GIRLTALK CHALLENGE

Do you have a situation in your life where it seems the BAD side of things is winning?

Take a cup of goodness, kindness, forgiveness and understanding into that situation and make a decision to show those things in action.

For example, send good wishes in a card, send a gift or flowers or home baking, making sure your intentions are honest and pure.

Do it with no expectation other than to be kind and to be a blessing in a difficult situation and I believe you will benefit greatly from doing 'a good thing'.

Good always wins in the end if you give it an opportunity to do so.

Your trials can become your treasure

We all have trials in our lives and need to understand each trial (or difficult time) can be a great time of learning. Approach it with understanding, work your way through it, step by step and you will get out the other side better for the experience.

- Learn how to examine the facts carefully and develop a successful strategy. Removing emotion while developing your plan will help a great deal. Stay calm during the trial. Do not over-react – add a little time into the equation if the situation allows.
- Every situation and circumstance you find yourself in has a strategy available to you - take the time to work it out and approach it with a balanced attitude.
- Each trial has a lesson. If you focus on the lesson and see it as an opportunity to grow, you will come through the trial more quickly and more effectively, but you must keep a positive and determined frame of mind! Keep telling yourself "I will get through this!" Every trial has a PURPOSE.
- Keep communication open and honest. Dishonesty will delay the process.
- Trials do have the potential to become a treasure in your life. This takes a high level of honesty with yourself and others.

Your trial becomes treasure when you have an opportunity to share what you have experienced with others, so your experience helps them through a similar experience. The treasure then becomes a thing of great value for you to offer others. The trial then has contributed something positive to your character and to the world. If you take this approach as you walk through life, you end up with a treasure chest instead of a pile of junk.

Personal Comment:

I have had many trials over the years. I can honestly say many of them have indeed become my treasure. Not all; I am still working on some, but I have a clear understanding of this principle and it does work.

When you have worked through a trial, conquered it and come out the other side willing to share it with others, you have your valuable precious treasure. Trials can be particularly painful to work through but when you do, you regain your power in that area of your life and so it has the making of beautiful treasure.

Turning my trials into treasure has now become one of my favourite things to do. Life will always have trials; that is life, but it's what we do with them that counts.

Some of my trials have been

- Sudden deaths of family members
- Divorce/broken relationships
- Rejection by people I love
- Being mistreated and wrongly judged
- Health issues.

No one can take your treasure from you, only you can give it away.

I am not saying I am an expert in these things but I believe when you have walked these paths you are given insight and understanding which can be helpful to others.

Heather says
"Your experiences are your treasure"

GIRLTALK CHALLENGE

Choose a trial you have been through and write down all the things you learnt from it. Then apply a thankful attitude to what you have learnt and begin to polish the lesson until it shines - then it will become something of value.

Share your trial and the things you have learnt from it with someone else. Share it in such a way the person will see the treasure you are offering. When the person you have shared this experience with walks away feeling valued and uplifted, you will know you have turned your trial into treasure.

Your treasure will then shine brightly into the lives of others.

This is one of the most significant Girltalk Challenges. If you can do this, you are truly a Girltalk Girlfriend.

Bless You,
Heather

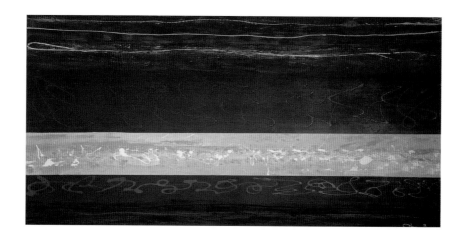

PAIN TO PRAISE

A story of a journey being worked out for the better

Keep a little mystery

- Do not give everything of yourself to people.
- Do not over-expose yourself; be careful and discreet, especially when experiencing new things and new people.
- Always hold a little back to create mystery.
- Know discretion is advisable - remember it's too late once it's out there.
- Keep something just for yourself. It is important to how you think about yourself.
- A wise woman knows it is not appropriate to show and tell all at once. Having a little mystery and intrigue about you can be a very attractive quality, without it being secretive, kooky or weird. (Mystery is not secrecy.)
- Be careful not to over-expose yourself with people you don't know or cannot trust. When revealing intimate details about yourself choose only your closest friends or family. Even then be careful; ask yourself if it's really necessary. Not everyone will understand your situation or treat it with the appropriate courtesy and respect.
- Be careful not to fall into the trap of thinking you should tell more than you are comfortable with. Some people have a knack of extracting information from others. Watch out for these people. You cannot trust them with confidences or private personal matters.
- Respect yourself enough to know it's OK not to tell everything.
- Mystery can be a good thing - but keep it in balance.

Be wary of people who ask too many questions about your private life when you have just met. (Actually, this really irritates me! I have an inbuilt alarm system that goes off when people do this.)

Personal Comment:

I recently had an experience with a lovely friend during a coffee. We had known each other approximately a year (not long really), had a mutual respect for each other and always enjoyed each other's company when we were together.

During our discussion she said lightly, "You know Heather, I really don't know very much about you. I am only just discovering more and more as time goes by."

My initial reaction was 'Is that a good thing or a bad thing?' Then I quickly realised this was a good thing as I had not over-exposed myself to her too soon and perhaps this was why our relationship was developing so well - it is always a rewarding experience when we are together.

Girls, seriously, we love to talk – it's what we do! But all 'talk' is not necessarily good for you. Guard your tongue. Do not let it be loose when talking about your personal life or the personal lives of people you love and care about.

HEATHER SAYS
"LESS IS MORE, UNTIL YOU ARE SURE"

GIRLTALK CHALLENGE

During discussion with friends practise holding back a little information.

Stop yourself just blabbing everything without thinking. Ask yourself "Do I really trust these people with all I say?"

Learn to hold your tongue. You don't have to say everything that enters your head.

Don't let your thoughts just roll off your tongue. Somewhere between thinking about it and speaking it, pause and check. If in doubt, don't let it out.

G

MAJESTY

The majesty and mystery of the mountains, sea and sky

Let go and move on

Letting go of our negative experiences and moving on from the past is the way to a better future. Have the courage to make the appropriate changes to achieve it. (I know this is terribly difficult sometimes, but we really need to do this girls! It will be worth it.)

- Have the courage to draw the line between your past and your future.
- Your future does not have to be determined by your past or even by your present circumstances.
- What has happened to you is not who you are. You are much more than what has happened to you.
- Understand the power of letting go and releasing 'stuff', moving away from it, leaving it behind. It is important not to allow negative aspects of your past to interfere with your way forward to better things. Letting go of something creates space and an opportunity for something better. You need to be disciplined emotionally and mentally to do it, but the courage to do it comes from an understanding of the reward and result that goes hand in hand with letting go. When you understand and believe something better is ahead for you, when you release the past and make a way for that better thing to come in your life, you will find the emotional and mental strength to do what you know you have to. Bring yourself to the point of being determined to go on. Make a decision, choose a better life – be free of your past.
- Do not hold on to negative experience but choose to be free of that which has hurt you.
- Life happens and things happen – it's the same for each and every one of us. How we process it and let it go determines our strength of character and our future. This particular principle of letting go is a key to living a life of freedom and joy. 'Stuff' happens to us all – the difference between us is what we choose to do with it.

- Positive 'letting go' affirmations are very helpful in working through, depending on the circumstances. Keep sheer determination and a positive faith and belief in yourself at all times, not giving up when you feel overwhelmed by what happened. Surround yourself with supportive people who will help you let go and move on, people who love you and believe in you and the amazing future awaiting you. Find someone you can talk to in confidence to help you. You don't have to do this alone!
- Develop a new plan, so you can focus on something fresh and stimulating e.g. something creative will bring new life back into your soul – e.g. decorating, gardening, painting, sewing, writing, learning something new or re-educating yourself, singing, dancing, music.

Examples of positive 'Letting Go' affirmations:

- I release myself from the past and walk freely into my future.
- I am leaving the past behind, from this day forward I begin anew.
- I draw a line between my past and future. What happened to me is not who I am.
- I will not take my negative experience from the past into my future.
- My future is free of my past and my future is full of goodness for me.
- I am strong and I have faith in myself and in God to overcome, and I have a great life ahead of me.
- I forgive myself and others for mistakes that have been made.

Make up your own 'letting go' affirmations specific to your circumstance, but remember, be kind and gentle to yourself.

If you need professional help to move on, get the help. Seek out someone who can support you to move on with confidence and a new vision. Don't waste any more time. Do it now.

Personal Comment:

From my own experience and through supporting many women over many years, I know the letting go and moving on process is one of the most difficult things for us to do. Even though externally a woman can seem to be moving on, internally she may still be trapped by her past. Being caught in the emotional trauma of a past event can have a very strong hold.

Talking with someone you trust is an important part of moving on and breaking that hold. Talking with my husband about my past ordeals was very healing for me. He just listened and loved me. He didn't judge me or focus on my mistakes. He focused on being a good listener, so I could release and talk out some of the things that were still hurting me. Voicing them aloud was very helpful to me, as if voicing them took their power away and released their hold on me.

Voicing them also helped me to laugh about some of my experiences; then I could sometimes make corny jokes about them and my husband and I could laugh. This was good medicine for me. If you have a husband or partner you can trust with your feelings, he could be a good choice to be your listening board, but it doesn't necessarily have to be him. It can be a counsellor, a parent, a sibling, or a friend – but be careful who you choose. Remember you need this person to LISTEN.

This is all about what is good for you during this exercise. Take as long as you need to; don't be hurried.

But there comes a time when even the talking about the past must stop, and the focus on a new plan needs to begin.

Be free, my darling girlfriend – Your PAST is history and Your FUTURE awaits you! Actually, because life just keeps on happening and people hurt people, I now make it a policy to just talk about stuff as it happens, so I don't carry it too long and before it gets down too deep.

HEATHER SAYS
"YOUR PAST IS HISTORY – MOVE INTO YOUR FUTURE
WITH FREEDOM"

GIRLTALK CHALLENGE

Take something negative from your past that lingers in the background of your life. Bring it into full focus and speak to it.

Tell it it no longer deserves space in your life and from this day remove its power to have any influence.

Shut the door on it and move into your future without it. Get appropriate help or support if you need help to do this. Don't waste any more precious time on it, you have a fabulous future waiting!

"Forgetting those things which are behind and reaching forward to those things which are ahead." **PHILIPPIANS 3:13**[6]

The art of timing

An acute awareness and understanding of the importance of timing gives a big advantage to those who have these skills – knowing when to move forward and when to stand still. This is more important than most people realise. Many a great idea has been sabotaged through inappropriate timing.

- View the horizon, gather information, explore the facts and use wisdom. (Knowledge, experience, understanding, common sense and insight are all important to the art of timing.)
- Trust the 'knowing' part of you to let you know when to move and when to stand still. This is a powerful gift you have been given; using it respectfully can be an enormous help in decision-making. Many of us make the mistake of rushing in before it is the right time. Others procrastinate and the opportunity is lost.

Although moving forward in life is part of a successful journey, there are times when being still and having a time of reflection is also useful.

- Deliberate moments of stillness and procrastination are two entirely different things.
- Procrastination is not being still. Procrastination is 'putting off' an action whose appropriate time is now.
- Stillness is a time of resting, reflecting, reviewing and re-establishing the path forward.
- Rushing ahead out of time can spoil many a good idea and plan.

Being patient is part of a successful process. It is part of our human nature to want to rush into things. Be willing to WAIT for confirmation and the 'knowing' which tells you now would be a good time. Move positively and decisively when you sense the time is right. Try not to be doubtful and hesitant once your decision is made and you believe your timing. Move forward without hesitation and doubt.

Successful people understand the Art of Timing and the seasons that go with timing. The right time is not necessarily a date, a time, a place – it is often a 'season', for example, this month, this year, this summer.

Personal Comment:

In my opinion, our biggest mistake as women is 'rushing in' and the mistake I see men make most often is procrastination (my personal view only). Hopefully between the two of us we can help each other with timing. I know my husband slows me down at times and at times I rev him up, so it works for us most of the time. Although I am sure I annoy him at times with my lack of patience, he is very gracious and calmly slows me down without discouraging me.

As I have grown older, I have become more disciplined with 'waiting, waiting, waiting' then moving on something. In the past, I would have perhaps waited, but not long enough – or just jumped right on in. Actually there was a time when I would have never waited, I would have just jumped in left, right and centre.

You can learn the art of timing. I have found discipline and patience to be major components - something I have had to work hard at, especially the patience part.

Remember "there is a time for everything under the sun". That includes all the things you want to do. The things you know in your heart are important to you will have their time and season. There is a time for you, your desires and your dreams.

Heather says
"Your time will come"

GIRLTALK CHALLENGE

Look ahead and consider when your Season and Time might be for each of the important things you want to happen in your life.

Begin to plan, prepare and position yourself well, so you can take full advantage of your opportunity at the right time.

Be careful not to miss your time.

GROUNDED

Keep yourself grounded at all times

Expectation and expansion

"Remember you are where you are in life because of what you believe you are worthy of." **OPRAH WINFREY**[10]

That statement should provoke some serious and honest thought: What do you believe you are worthy of? It is out of that place, you decide what will happen in your life. You are making decisions unconsciously and consciously from this belief system. Understand YOU are responsible for where you are today because of past decisions. Please don't feel guilty about that, just recognise it. We have all made helpful and unhelpful decisions – that's life and learning.

What you are expecting will be what you create, so be honest with yourself about what you truly believe you are worth. What are you honestly and truthfully expecting to happen?

"Where your thoughts go, your life will follow"
JOYCE MEYER[5]

Examine yourself and ask what you truly believe you are worth. Where does your self worth lie on a scale of one to ten? Don't be too hard on yourself, but be honest, then begin to move your worth up the scale to reach 10 (if it's not already there) because that's where you deserve to be.

What you are expecting is what you will get. Analyse what you are expecting. Write a list of what you believe you are worth in different areas of your life e.g. career, health, relationships, children. Be honest with yourself and make changes you realise are required. Expect something wonderful. It may be difficult and seem strange to begin with, but keep at it. The things which seem impossible today may be possible tomorrow.

Begin to believe good things happen to you and will continue to happen to you. Expect them to happen because you deserve them. Everyone deserves good things to happen to them. That's the truth!

Here again is the Power and the Opportunity of Choice.
The choice to expect and believe…or not.
Are you expecting something positive…or something negative?
Are you expecting something big and great…or are you expecting something small and insignificant?

DEFINITION:
Expansion[11] - development, enlargement, evolution, increase, magnification, maturation, spread, stretch, unfurling.

If you expect greater things in your life, then you must expect to have expansion. Are you prepared for expansion? Have you made room for expansion? Do you have a plan for expansion? Be clear on what direction you want to go in. It is very difficult to expand without knowing what area or areas of your life you are trying to enlarge.

Create your plan for expansion, your expectation for expansion.
For example,

- expand your experience
- expand your knowledge
- expand your influence
- expand your effectiveness
- expand your fruitfulness
- expand your prosperity
- expand your career
- expand your family

Expansion is a lot of fun and it is also part of evolving as a person, finding what you are capable of and continuously moving towards greater potential.

Personal Comment:

Dear Girlfriends,

A few years ago, my self worth would have been around four on the scale. I have now moved it up to about nine. It has taken me some time to get there, but it certainly is a valuable thing to work on. Good luck to you.

I discovered a number of years ago the power of what we expect to happen in our lives. That is why I keep a very active visualisation and faith programme. These are the things I am EXPECTING TO HAPPEN.

My dreams and aspirations over the years have shifted the focus from what benefits me to what I can do now to benefit others. I prayerfully consider my expectations, then when I am comfortable with what I am expecting, I totally believe and begin to plan for my expectations to be met.

I have expectations bursting in my heart and mind to do significant things to help others have a better life. I have expanded beyond my own need. As I am beginning to do these things I myself am expanding and growing rapidly and being challenged along the way. It's a wonderful time and a wonderful place to be.

Heather says
"Expand your expectation"

GIRLTALK CHALLENGE

Make a list of things you are expecting to grow in.

Why not begin to consider positive expansion, and plan for it?

I encourage you to expand your expectation beyond yourself and your present circumstance. Begin to believe you are worthy and capable of great things.

Allow yourself to expect the unexpected to happen to you. Know you deserve the best. Believe you are worthy of a big, full and wonderful life.

EXPECT it to happen.

Visualise your dreams

It helps to use your imagination to help you visualise your dreams. Our mind thinks in pictures, not words e.g. if I say "the ocean", those of us who have seen the ocean will 'picture' it in our minds when we hear the word. Our mind does not go O.C.E.A.N (the word and letters); we visualise the beautiful blue ocean, so for most of us our mind works in pictures.

It has been said we move towards that which we think about and if our minds think in pictures, we need to be picturing or visualising beautiful things we want to happen for ourselves and others. Create a picture in your mind of your dreams and passionately believe in them. Capture the picture, like a snapshot and keep it in your view.

Believing is the KEY. All things are possible to those who believe. Passionately believe and visualise your dreams. If it helps you to visualise your dreams, cut out pictures of them and place them where you can see them on a regular basis. This will keep you focused and keep your believing active.

You move towards that which you believe in and think about.

PERSONAL COMMENT:

Obviously common sense needs to be applied here, but I personally know visualising my dreams plays an enormous part in achieving them. Don't be discouraged by people who say it is nonsense. Those people are dream killers. If you can't see it, how can you achieve it? So create beautiful pictures in your mind to focus on your dreams.

I have found it personally helpful to write down important things I would like to achieve before I die. I don't want to have regrets when I reach an age where I may no longer be able to do the things I wished I had. I want to feel I have done well and I have done all I could, with the opportunities I was given.

I visualise almost every important thing I want to achieve. I also visualise in full colour and the picture I visualise is one which brings me and others a lot of joy and blessing. I even visualise other people receiving a blessing from MY dream. Once I have the picture in my mind and my heart I start with the smallest piece of the puzzle, then work my way to fitting all the pieces together, keeping my dream clearly in view, until it is complete.

If your dream changes along the way, that's okay! Sometimes it is a process of evolution to get there. Try it, it's a lot of fun and easier than you think. It's a choice, followed by action. Don't settle for less than your dreams.

HEATHER SAYS
"CREATE BEAUTIFUL, COLOURFUL PICTURES IN YOUR MIND"

GIRLTALK CHALLENGE

Cut out pictures of your dreams. Make a pictureboard of your dreams and keep it where you can see it on a regular basis. Do it with friends or family have fun with it. Visualise yourself in the picture.

Allow yourself to believe you are worthy of this dream. Because you ARE.

Leave a legacy

Here's a question for you to ponder: when you are gone, what will you leave behind?

How do you want to be remembered? Do you want your life to have made a difference outside of yourself? Will your life speak of something significant for the future generations? Will the world benefit in some way from your being here? What is your legacy dream in your heart?

It's good to begin to think of these things while you still have time. Plan and begin to establish your legacy.

Choose one thing to begin with and make it happen. It doesn't matter how small it is – a small ripple goes a long way on a large pond. Planning to leave something behind which changed someone else's life for the better, to give something to someone who couldn't do it for themselves, is very significant; significant in a way we may never know.

Your legacy can be whatever you want it to be. Maybe it's about your children or grandchildren – or someone else's - maybe it's a community thing, maybe it's planting a tree. There are no rules for leaving a legacy; it's simply imparting something of what you have, to leave a person, a situation or a place better than it was.

A legacy does not necessarily need money; there are countless ways to help others and to make a lasting difference in situations. Most of us will have something in our lives which can be used to leave a legacy. Use what you have been blessed with to enhance the lives of other people. A legacy can be established by utilising a natural talent we have, a position or influence we have to help others. Every person's legacy will be different but equally important to the world.

Personal Comment:

My desire to leave a legacy certainly got me motivated. It has changed my life and I love it! I started with small things and believe doing them for others with unconditional love in my heart, is leaving a legacy.

One of my dreams for a legacy was wanting to do something for orphans and widows.

> "....to look after orphans and widows in their distress"
> **JAMES 1:27[8]**

This year I was able to fund the building of a home in Uganda for orphans and widows (photos on next page.) The orphanage home concept means homes are built to create a home for orphans and widows to live together in family units. Homes where children have a mother and a woman has children. Homes based on love and support, not just providing a roof and food.

This concept stole my heart and I had no peace until I built one of these homes to take care of these beautiful people. Visit http://www.watoto.com for more information.

This is the most significant legacy I have left so far – it makes me feel as if my life mattered for someone else, somewhere on the planet. My contribution could, in some way, end up changing lives for countless numbers of people over time. How amazing is that? What a privilege I have.

I believe this will end up being one of the most important things to me from here on – the desire to ensure I leave a legacy for others less fortunate than me and to teach my family to do the same.

I also intend to use some of the profits from the sale of this book to support other women. I have formed "The Girltalk Foundation" and will put some of the profits into it, for distribution to charities which support women and children.

HEATHER SAYS
"LEAVE A LEGACY OF LOVE"

GIRLTALK CHALLENGE

You can begin to establish a legacy today.

Your legacy can be anything you want it to be, but one that improves the lives of others is by far the best kind.

Begin with small things to change people's lives for the better.

You can leave just one legacy or many – it's up to you, but I encourage you to leave at least one. Imagine if every person left just one legacy to help those less fortunate, what a different world we would live in.

Don't miss out on the awesome privilege of leaving a legacy.

Health and Wellbeing

BODY, SOUL & SPIRIT

Three in one

The 3 DU - body, soul and spirit

If you don't understand how you are made and how you work, you will find it difficult to live your true life, reach your full potential and fulfil your destiny. Once you know how you 'tick' then you can begin to take charge of your life.

You are a Body, a Soul and a Spirit. All three parts of you are critical to your health and wellbeing.

Our Body is the vehicle in which we move around and this is what the world sees and interacts with. Healthy eating, exercise and rest/sleep are important to help our body perform well.

Our Soul is our *mind*, our *will* and our *emotions*; our thinking, our will and our feelings. Healthy and supportive thoughts, self control and balanced emotions contribute to a soul's wellbeing.

Our Spirit is the REAL person, the invisible you. Your spirit is the most beautiful part of you, the part of you which knows your true purpose. A healthy spirit is connected to God the Creator, for He and He alone is the source of our spiritual wellbeing. Your spirit understands who you are in the world and what you are here for.

The three parts of us are perfectly designed to work together in harmony. So when one part gets out of balance, things may not go so well – for example, if we allow ourselves to be ruled by our emotions we will make many mistakes because emotions and feelings are not dependable or reliable. Usually all three parts need consideration in all we do.

Body:

- Is your physical body in good health?
- Are you energetic and strong?
- Is your body ready to accomplish the things you need it to do?

Soul:

- Do you have all the information you need?
- Do you have the will to do it?
- Are your emotions in good health and well balanced?

Spirit:

- Are you listening to your spirit?
- Does your spirit (the REAL you) agree with your body and soul?
- Are your three parts in agreement? Do you have unity and peace?

If you have considered all these things, you are well balanced and ready.

Personal Comment:

Once I began to understand this, it helped me enormously – especially when dealing with my soul. I'm learning to let my spirit rule. I can trust my spirit more than my soul, though my soul is helpful. When I understand what I am thinking and feeling, and keep those things in check and on the right track, my soul contributes positively.

We really are amazing creations. Learning about myself and how I tick is a never-ending journey. Though there is a lot of information on this subject, my personal best source for body, soul and spirit is my bible.

It's time to understand who we really are – a body, a soul and a spirit. All three parts need nurturing for us to be balanced, healthy and whole in every way.

I personally find my soul needs a lot of care to stay in truth and balance, especially the emotional side of my soul, but now I have some understanding of it, I stay tuned in to my spirit for the truth.

Learning to love myself in a healthy way and give myself the attention I need is something I am understanding more and more. I am learning to be kind and gentle to myself, which is quite a new thing for me, as I would say I am more demanding on myself than kind. But that is changing every day!

Two people who have helped me with understanding this are Joyce Meyer and Glenna Salsbury. I recommend their writing to you –

"The Art of the Fresh Start" by Glenna Salsbury (www.glennasalsbury.com)

"Spirit, Soul and Body" Teaching Series by Joyce Meyer (www.joycemeyer.org)

HEATHER SAYS
"LOVE YOUR BODY, SOUL AND SPIRIT"

GIRLTALK CHALLENGE

Spend some time on this subject and let it settle. Once you see yourself as three parts, you will begin to understand how to manage yourself to your full potential.

I encourage you to study this subject for further understanding, perhaps through reading the books I have recommended.

Be kind and gentle to yourself every day in some way and I pray that all will go well with you.

Establish and maintain healthy boundaries

A great life cannot be achieved if we allow negative and destructive things into our lives, things we know should not be there, areas of compromise and imbalance. I believe we all have some of these things in different areas of our lives from time to time, but unhealthy compromise keeps us from the best and keeps us from being awake to new opportunities coming our way.

Most people see boundaries as being restricting or limiting but I don't see them that way at all! When you truly understand what a healthy boundary looks like, you realise it creates more freedom and allows good things to come your way. In fact, establishing and maintaining healthy boundaries can be very liberating and create freedom for you to live your own life and make your own choices without pressure from others.

- Establishing a boundary means drawing a line between what is acceptable to you and what is not acceptable to you and clearly defining the two – then ceasing participation in that which is not acceptable to you, your beliefs and values.
- Establishing a boundary requires clear balanced thinking, courage and discipline.
- Healthy boundaries allow you to keep out of your life things which are not good for you – things which distract you from your best life.
- Healthy boundaries in particular areas of your life will prevent you from being cheated out of a greater reward e.g. sexual boundaries, financial, emotional, physical, spiritual or communication boundaries.
- Boundaries will enhance your life greatly in many ways, which puts you in a better position to enhance the lives of others.
- Have the courage to make decisions and appropriate changes where and when required.
- Have the discipline to implement changes, even against resistance.

- Have the perseverance to stick to the task when others want you to opt out for their sake, not yours.

People pursuing a 'great life' clearly understand life is a consequence of previous choices and we can change the future by making different choices to those made in the past. Begin to establish and maintain healthy boundaries to begin the journey to be free from other people's expectations, so you can live your life and fulfil your destiny without interference from others.

Boundaries need to be established around each relationship to ensure the relationship flourishes in a manner, so it can be maintained long-term.

- Unhealthy boundaries allow people to occupy spaces in our lives they don't belong in.
- It's important to understand who we are as separate and defined individuals.
- It's important to understand the difference between playing an enhancing role in each other's lives and that where one person is dominant and controlling.
- An unhealthy boundary is one which leaves you feeling frustrated and powerless.

Women often do not establish boundaries in relationships with one another; then find themselves being taken advantage of.

- It is supportive to gently pull back to establish a healthy boundary in a relationship.
- Courage, discipline and perseverance go with boundaries.

Action Points for Healthy Boundaries:

- Make your OWN decisions without pressure or influence from others.
- Communication boundaries are vital.
- Put boundaries around who you will (and won't) discuss private matters with.
- Politely say NO to things and people you are not comfortable with.

Without boundaries we put ourselves into circumstances where we will eventually be let down, hurt or offended, by:

- Living a life largely influenced by wanting acceptance from others,
- Wanting to please everyone,
- Not being comfortable saying NO, without having to justify it,
- Being taken advantage of in the workplace,
- Over-giving of yourself (emotional and physical) and of material things.

Personal Comment:

There was a time when I would give more of myself and my time to those around me, so they would think highly of me, value me and include me. This led to people feeling obligated to me, though I did not intend that to happen and was not aware of it at the time.

Even though I am in a position to give generously in many areas of my life, I have learned it is not always wise. I had an overwhelming desire to meet the needs of others wherever and whenever the situation arose. At the time I believed it was the right thing to do because I could. I now understand this type of over-giving is unhealthy for everyone. I believe relationships should be of equal giving and receiving. When I began to understand this behaviour, I made a conscious decision to place a boundary around an acceptable amount of giving of myself to others.

I also had to establish boundaries to protect myself from people wanting to control and manipulate me to enhance their own position or get my support in an inappropriate way. I have now learned the happy balance of boundaries and understand their importance to living my life freely – and letting others do the same.

Give yourself an honest answer

- Is my life well balanced, or do one or two things dominate?
- Do I have trouble understanding when to say no?
- Do I feel pressured into saying yes when I know I should be saying no?
- Am I feeling stressed, exhausted, and overcome by my circumstances?
- Do I feel guilty about setting clear boundaries to protect myself, my dreams and my goals?
- Am I fully aware of the circumstances and the consequences and situations I find myself in?
- Do I go back and forth on matters, perhaps yielding to other people's opinions?
- Am I prepared to make sacrifice and change to have more peace and pleasure in my life?
- Do I feel confident about who I am and what I believe in?

If you truly want balance and freedom to live life well, these questions need honest answers – and probably some changes to be made. However, don't beat yourself up over things these questions may bring to the surface. Just consider each one and calmly decide whether any action is required.

Personal Comment:

As you can see, it will take time to answer each question honestly, process your responses and make decisions about any change required. I have personally discovered that by considering these things carefully and being boundary conscious I have less stress in my life. I enjoy life more, because there is less confusion and misunderstanding from others.

It's liberating when people around you understand and respect your boundaries. It also helps them establish theirs.

Areas we need boundaries

Physical, Intellectual, Emotional, Spiritual, Financial, Communication

Clearly understanding what is appropriate – and what is not – in each of these different areas of your life, is vital to living as the person you are supposed to be and not what others want or expect. Take the time to consider each of these areas:

Physical - Are there people in your life you have physical contact with, with whom you are not comfortable? It is very important to only allow people YOU want to touch you to do so. Some people will impose themselves on you physically and sexually. Establish a firm boundary in this area. Do not put yourself in positions of risk. e.g. being alone with people you don't trust, or over-exposing your body. Learn the art of body language so you do not give out the wrong message.

Intellectual - Are there people in your life who influence your thoughts and opinions in a different direction than the one you believe in? Listening to the opinions of others is good, but be sure you are still in control of your own thoughts and opinions and establishing them on a sound basis.

Emotional - Are there people in your life who have a negative impact on your emotions or make you feel less than adequate when you are around them? Be wary of people who upset and hurt you, make critical comments, subtly undermine you to make themselves look better.

Spiritual - Are there people in your life who make you feel unworthy, impose their will upon you spiritually and interfere with your personal relationship with God? Do not allow others to come between you and God. Your relationship with God is private and personal to you. Do not allow people to undermine your faith or make you feel less worthy than you are. God loves you unconditionally just the way you are.

Financial – Boundaries on finances are very important. Budgeting is a must and sticking to it is vital. Do not allow yourself to be controlled by financial debt. Have a good financial plan in place and guard this area of your life carefully.

Communication – Boundaries on communication are important so as not to mislead people, or have them misunderstand your intentions. Be very clear about your intent and what you say. A communication boundary also involves you, as the 'listener', putting a stop to any conversation you believe is inappropriate. This may mean removing yourself from the environment in which the conversation is taking place.

Personal Comment:

I first learned about the concept of boundaries some years ago at an International Women's Conference in the USA. During this conference I realised I was living my life without clear boundaries. It was an enormous revelation to me and I began to understand why certain things kept happening to me. Establishing boundaries was something I had never been taught or heard of.

To this day I am still developing boundaries. It is an ongoing process because life is a journey and we are forever changing, as are our circumstances. So for me now it is something I consider on a regular basis and make adjustments as I go. This may all sound just too much, but don't let it overwhelm you. Consider each area of your life carefully, then, one step at a time implement any changes to help you put a boundary between that which is healthy for you and that which is not. Get advice or help from others if you need support to put your boundaries in place. Boundaries really do help everyone, even the people who think they don't need them.

Recommended Reading: 'Boundaries' by Dr Henry Cloud and Dr John Townsend. Zondervan Publishing (1992)

Heather says
"Everyone wins with boundaries"

GIRLTALK CHALLENGE

I've posed a lot of questions for you in this section.

Start with one question and answer it, considering carefully what you need to do in that situation to take back control of your life.

Set a healthy boundary, remembering to do it with subtlety and respect so as not to cause upset to others who may be affected by your boundary setting.

Remember, one little step at a time when making changes will help the transition go more smoothly and you will be more likely to maintain it long-term.

The art of pause

P…A…U…S…E.
Take in a slow deliberate breath.
B…R…E…A…T…H…E.

Breathing in slowly and deliberately is very helpful to us if we do it regularly throughout the day. Focus on inhaling slowly through your nose, feeling the air travel up your nostrils, keep inhaling until you feel the air pushing your tummy out, hold the breath, then let it out through your mouth with gentle control. This seems to unwind tension and bring you back to the centre. When I do this I try to 'God Centre' myself, connect with God, before moving on.

Pausing to breathe slowly feels gentle and nurturing and is another part of caring for myself. In moments of pause, ideas come, thoughts evolve, the Spirit speaks, healing occurs, wisdom reveals itself. The pause might seem like a fleeting moment, but some of the most profound things have happened to me in my time of pause. 'Pause' is a good word and even better when you action it. Just the mention of the word triggers something in me to immediately start to breathe more slowly to 'God Connect'.

PERSONAL COMMENT:

Pausing is something I am very aware of these days, after spending many years racing around.

We seem to have to learn to P…A…U…S…E. I recently read an article saying we were all walking faster, talking faster and eating faster.

I think this may be true and I don't find it very attractive.

To pause regularly throughout my day has helped me enjoy myself more and helped me take time to be kind to myself. As women, particularly those of us in our second half of life, The Art of Pause is important to have moments of joy. When I think about the word menopause and break it down I wonder: Men–o–pause. One thing I do know is if we don't learn to pause and slow down regularly, life will make us do it in other ways. It is better to make the decision to do this for ourselves.

I call it the Art of Pause, because I believe most of us have to learn how to do this in such a way it becomes a gift to us.

HEATHER SAYS
"PAUSE AND FEEL THE JOY"

GIRLTALK CHALLENGE

Set the alarm on your watch or cellphone to go off every hour during your day for a few days and when it rings …. STOP and PAUSE for a few moments (maybe 30 seconds).

Breathe slowly, connect with yourself.

I am sure you will begin to love these moments, as I do.

The importance of health

Health must have high priority if you are to live your life to the full potential you have within you. Health and wellbeing is the answer to living out our lives from beginning to end magnificently, having health and vitality to fulfil our potential and live our dreams. I have discovered when I feel well, healthy and strong, I enjoy everything so much more and I definitely have more FUN.

Health is a lifestyle choice. Considering the long-term advantages of healthy living is important when you make today's decisions about health. Invest in your future health by making disciplined and wise choices now. Health does not have to be obsessive or overly demanding. Food, exercise and rest are three critical factors in health. I realise there are other factors in some cases, but for most of us, these three elements are what make the difference.

Let's start with **food**. Educate yourself on what makes a well balanced diet. This does not have to be complicated; just good common sense eating will give you the best results; fresh is best, green is great, and keep quantities to a minimum. Most of us eat more than we need. I believe the most common health-related mistake is the quantities and portions of the food eaten. Little and often is really the best for us, keeping our bodies fuelled but not stuffed, keeping our metabolism running higher and keeping our energy levels high. Eating slowly helps us realise we don't need as much as we think. It takes a few minutes for our brain to register we have had enough.

If you want your body to be different, make firm decisions regarding this and change what you are eating. Don't make food decisions with your eyes, make them before the food gets in front of you. Plan your food in advance and stick to it. Remember, the spirit is willing but the flesh is weak. (Oh, how I know this!)

We women spend far too much time worrying about our weight and starting new diets. If we put this energy into re-educating ourselves and changing our beliefs and behaviours regarding food choices, we might just find a happy balance with our health and weight.

We really are what we eat, so do yourself a favour and get help if you have an obsession with food. If you have an emotional eating problem, acknowledge it and get help. It's important to work out why you are over or under-eating and tackle the real problem.

YOU ARE WHAT YOU EAT – it's true. I am an emotional eater at times. If I am tired or stressed, I eat chocolate. I always regret it because the pleasure is not worth the regret. Emotional eating is not the same as making a balanced decision to have a little treat for pleasure.

Keep alcohol intake to a minimum, eliminate smoking and recreational drug use. Don't pollute your body; it's a masterpiece and polluting it is not very smart. Don't take anything into your body that destroys it. It's that simple; we have created many of our health issues, so only we can begin to reverse the effects. Your body has an amazing ability to renew itself. All is not lost, so let's get cracking! The choice is yours.

Women so often cheat themselves of wellbeing in areas of health. Women who choose health are well disciplined. They understand food, alcohol, smoking, or drug use can be used as a crutch or an excuse for not dealing with other issues. Don't be afraid to deal with issues in your life – especially ones leading you to make unhealthy life style choices. Come on girls! We know better and we deserve better.

Exercise is important to maintaining good body function. You must plan and schedule this into your day and week. View it as an appointment with your body and your future health. Don't make excuses; you will be so pleased with yourself when you exercise regularly. The benefits far outweigh any effort you put in.

Everyone has the opportunity to exercise. Walking doesn't cost you anything, doesn't require anyone else, you can do it with or without children, you can do it early in the morning or late in the evening or any time in between. You simply must make it a priority.

Exercise is critical to overall health, fitness, strength, muscle tone, weight, stress, hormone balance. Walk, swim, jog, cycle, go to the gym, take up a sport. Just do it, you will love yourself for it! Do whatever works for you.

Sleep and Rest are other important health factors. No-one can burn the candle at both ends and stay on top for long. Lack of sleep will lead to many other problems in your life, so give yourself a break and start the day fresh and well rested.

Have a regular bed time and arise time so your body knows it can count on you to take care of it. It will perform well for you when you get ample sleep and rest. I have learnt my body simply will not perform for me without seven or eight hours' sleep every night. So I have become very disciplined with this because I have a very high expectation of myself - in my work and the purpose for my life. Sure, I can still take an odd late night when the occasion arises, but only when the occasion calls for it. Believe me, it must be worth it! I don't like wasting sleep time.

Another thing I have started doing in recent times is having a rest during the day. This only needs to be 20-30 minutes. Just sitting and being still for a short time, resting my mind and body – it's amazing how a short rest refreshes me!

I remove myself from the intensity of my work and just sit somewhere comfortable and warm, take my shoes off and close my eyes and rest my mind. Then I am ready to begin the rest of the day refreshed and refocused.

If you are unable to do this, take 10 minutes at your desk or in your car. I have been known to take my rest moments in some very strange places! The important thing is to recognise when your body, soul and spirit need a rest. It works beautifully and feels right to give yourself this time. Your body and mind will reward you for it. Do whatever it takes to have long term health and wellbeing – Choose a Great Life!

Personal Comment:

Firstly I would like to clarify I am not an expert in this field, but I now know what works for me and am blessed with wonderful health. I plan to live long and happily.

Please don't be too busy to take care of yourself properly. I made this mistake for many years. I worked like a machine and it was not worth it. It takes its toll. I am happy to say now I value my health, wellbeing, my body, soul and spirit and I give each of these things the time they deserve. The reward is I am a better person to be around! I believe my family would agree with that. In addition I have more joy, I am more creative, more connected with my purpose and the part my health plays in that.

I have learnt to pause and think carefully about the decisions I make when eating. Sometimes I still choose to have 'it', but other times I don't. The times when I choose not to are becoming more frequent as I become more aware of the health choices I am making when I am emotional or tired.

When I look back over the years, especially my teenage years, I realise now I was emotionally troubled and much of my eating was emotional over-eating. I am grateful I have figured out and taken control of this response I have to connecting food with my emotional state; e.g. when I get upset or angry, I eat, usually sweet things. It's almost self-sabotage.

My biggest challenge at present is the portion size of my eating. Smaller portions are critical for me when making food decisions. Exercise has always been important to me - I love the feeling of being hot and sweaty and pushing myself physically with exercise. Exercise clears my head, relaxes me and helps me feel more confident.

I am mindful to stay active and moving – there is still so much life to be had. In fact, I believe the best is still to come. Find some exercise you enjoy and do it! The way we treat our bodies and our general health will have the last say.

"Dear Friend, I pray that you may enjoy good health and that all may go well with you, even as your soul is getting along well" JOHN 3:2⁸

HEATHER SAYS
"BE HEALTH SMART!"

99

GIRLTALK CHALLENGE

Make a plan to write a checklist for your health.

List out the four categories: exercise, food, rest and recreation and write your wishlist under each one. Turn the wishlist into a "to do" list. Do yourself a big favour and stick with it.

Healthy girls have more fun!

BOUNDARIES

Clearly established boundaries bring health and wellbeing

Presenting the best you

Dressing appropriately and developing your style

We all have the potential to look beautiful, but some of us don't yet know how to make the best of ourselves. Understand:

- Your body shape and its proportions
- How to dress to correctly balance your body shape
- What to wear to which occasion (anything does NOT go)
- When it's appropriate to expose skin (and how much) and when it's not
- This is a big mistake many women make
- When a bra is necessary - most of the time actually
- The difference between evening and day wear
- The appropriate footwear for the clothing style
- The type of fabric for the article of clothing and the purpose of the garment

Wearing clothing or underwear which is too small for you is a major 'faux pas' many women make. Clothing which is too small makes you look bigger, because it clings to and emphasises the largest parts of us.

If need be, get guidance on how to dress appropriately. This is not about how much you can afford to spend on clothing, but knowing what to buy and what to choose from your wardrobe for all circumstances, so you can walk with confidence throughout your day and not be constantly thinking or worrying about your clothing or how you look. Feeling inadequate or embarrassed with the way you are dressed can ruin your day and your ability to perform and be at your best.

Keeping it simple and stylish always works best. Obviously there are occasions when dramatic and dynamic are appropriate, but mostly it's about developing a great style to suit you and work for you on a day-to-day basis, so you look wonderful every day, not just on special occasions.

If you have had an article of clothing for a long time, absolutely love it to bits and cannot bear to part with it, it probably is a good indication of your style and colour. Certain colours will work better for you than others, so identify them and let them work for you.

Style is more flattering than fashion, so learn how to put a little fashion into your style.

Develop and have a clearly defined style that relates to who you are. You don't need to be a 'fashion slave' or chop and change with the trends to always look current and stylish.

- Stay away from extreme.
- Style is more than what you wear; it's how you wear it and how you carry yourself with confidence.
- Style is being comfortable with who you are and how you feel on the inside.
- Style is knowing how to make the best of what you have got.
- Style is uniquely you and when you find your style, it will be the most attractive and most appealing look for you.
- Style is not copying someone else and not wishing you looked like someone else. Your style is about being the 'Best You'.

Think carefully about those favourite pieces of clothing you never want to throw out, the pieces that you feel great in. Think about the hair style and colour that make you feel your best. Think about all of the things in your life that please you and make you feel good about who you are - then you are on your way to recognising and developing your style.

Remember STYLE is about confidence in WHO YOU ARE, not only the way you look. TRUST YOURSELF AND FOLLOW YOUR HEART.

HEATHER SAYS
"KEEP IT SIMPLE AND YOUR STYLE WILL EMERGE"

A fresh hairstyle

Change your hairstyle regularly; do not get caught in a time warp. (We all know someone like this don't we, her hair looks the same as it did 20 years ago.) Check yourself and make sure you are not one of these people. Hanging onto an old hairstyle can mean you do not want to move on with your life and experience new things - maybe you are using your hair as a security blanket.

Keeping a fresh up-to-date hairstyle will make you look and feel younger - and more vibrant!

- Carefully choose your hair stylist and make sure you communicate clearly what you want, while being open to experienced advice. If you are not satisfied, change your hairdresser.
- Keep in mind that certain face shapes suit certain styles and certain skin tones suit certain colours e.g. long lean face shapes should avoid long straight hair, a person with a pink skin tone should avoid gold hair colours. Again make sure your stylist knows about this; not everyone wants the latest shape and colour regardless of their personal attributes.
- Choose a style you can manage easily yourself, to avoid only looking great when you have left the hair salon and not so great for the rest of time.
- Don't be afraid to cut long hair (it will grow). Unless long hair is beautifully groomed and maintained at all times it can really drag you down and look less than attractive. Opting for a shorter, more snappy style can give you a fresh, younger look if you don't have the time to keep long hair beautifully groomed.
- Same with colour; don't be afraid to try a new colour - it may just soften and enhance you, something we need to be mindful of as we grow older. (Bleached blonde and matt jet black are not good looks on anyone.)
- Even natural colour can be enhanced by a little colour to add shine and depth.
- Spending money on a good hair cut and colour is a good investment.

Do this regularly, don't skimp on this. Your hair can make or break your look and beautifully groomed hair can make you feel and look a million dollars.

Hair is something we girls think about quite a lot - cutting it, shaving it, waxing it, trimming it, plucking it, shampooing it, conditioning it and more.

The importance of grooming

Grooming yourself should be a priority. For example, hair, skincare, hands/feet, nails, makeup, hair removal, clean and pressed clothing, clean footwear.

- Invest time in yourself to maintain a high level of grooming. Most good basic grooming costs very little, only your time and commitment to yourself.
- Excellent grooming does matter; first impressions do count, people do notice and appreciate good grooming, so it will make a significant difference how people receive you. People notice the smallest of details e.g. dirty nails, soiled clothing, cuffs and collars.
- Don't think "It doesn't matter this time" because it does.
- You cannot over-groom yourself as far as cleanliness and neatness go, but be careful not to become obsessed.
- Your personal hygiene should be a high priority at all times.
- Never underestimate the importance of grooming. Don't let yourself believe "average is OK". Excellence in grooming is essential if you want to leave a great impression and feel confident.

Excellent grooming is also about loving and respecting yourself at all times; every day, not just when you have a 'hot date' or want to impress someone.

The most fabulous outfit will not get a second glance if your grooming is not up to the mark. People will overlook your fabulous outfit but will notice dirty hair, chipped nail polish, shabby shoes and so on.

PERSONAL COMMENT:

The most important piece of advice I believe I can give you is not to compare yourself to others. This may make you feel you don't measure up because we always see in others what we believe we don't have ourselves and it can leave us feeling inadequate. This is not true – every one of us has valuable and attractive assets. Developing your style will help you highlight these.

I keep my wardrobe to a few basic pieces each season, pieces I know work with my body shape and proportions, then work around those with extras. I personally can't be bothered with clothes I have to fuss with - I like to put something on in the morning and forget about it. This is an important part of style for me.

I recently had my long hair cut short after much deliberation. It's the best thing I have done in a long time ! Don't be afraid of change, it's only hair – it does grow! Keep it freshly cut and shiny. This is far more attractive than long unkempt hair. I found I was pulling my long hair into a ponytail most days, which was fine, but what was the point if it annoyed me when I wore it loose?

I believe that as we get older we need to choose styles which keep us looking fresh and be prepared to change our hairstyle regularly. If you haven't had a hairstyle change in the past two years, please consider it.

While we are talking about hair, do yourself a favour and have your eyebrows shaped professionally. A fresh hairstyle and shaped eyebrows frame your face and can make you look years younger. Don't underestimate the eyebrows, girls!

Love yourself enough to present the best you each day – not only for others, but for yourself. You will walk through your day with a high level of confidence if you prepare well before leaving home.

Don't forget about your shoes! Some of you may be thinking, this is very basic, but it has been my experience over decades of working with beautiful women that many girls do not give their grooming the time it deserves, and wonder why they don't get that second glance.

Know and like yourself

Discover who you are and be happy with yourself. You are unique, valuable and beautiful. Sometimes it takes a while to reach this place but when you do, it sure feels great to finally be there. Being kind and generous to yourself about who you are is an important part of allowing yourself to develop into the real you. Being negative about yourself will stop you from releasing the beautiful person you are inside. See yourself as having real value - because you do.

Total acceptance of yourself is a huge step forward. Not everyone reaches this place; many say they like and accept themselves, but really they do not, so be honest. It must be an honest heartfelt thing. The Real You is magnificent, beautiful, talented and lovely.

When you present the "real you" to others, they will love you because the "real you" represents the best of you.

- The real and natural you is the most attractive thing about you.
- The more you like and accept yourself (in a natural and healthy way) the more others will like and accept you. Don't be hard on yourself; you are a beautiful creative woman with lots to offer the world. Please allow yourself to be that person.
- Focus on your strengths; develop them and be proud of who you are and what you have to offer.

- Believe you are a kind, loving, generous, beautiful woman. Live in this belief and the 'Real You' will emerge magnificently. Remember, what has happened to you is not who you are. You truly are magnificent - you were from the beginning, still are and always will be!

How do you add value to the lives of others around you? Family, friends, colleagues, relatives and acquaintances. Decide what is appropriate for each situation and deposit something of your valuable self everywhere you go. This is an important part of the real you that is so attractive. You will discover by doing this, you will like yourself more and more and your beautiful spirit will show expression to the world around you. Discovering your value is important, but actually you have value just the way you are – you were born with value. Loving and valuing yourself is an important step to the REAL YOU emerging. Give the REAL YOU permission to stand up and step forward.

PERSONAL COMMENT:

I have discovered on my travels nationally and internationally that women everywhere have a tendency to not like themselves, or give themselves a high value.

They tend to say: "I am only…", "I am just a…", "I am not really important".

This was me until a few years ago when I discovered I am a nice person and I have value, not only to my family and friends, but I have something valuable and unique which no-one else can offer the world – ME.

Tell yourself regularly how much you like yourself (in a healthy way of course) and do things to make you feel good about yourself, if you need convincing. You really are a nice person without trying! Girls are gorgeous human beings - we bring beauty and balance in many ways.

HEATHER SAYS
"YOU ARE TRULY UNIQUE AND FABULOUS!"

GIRLTALK CHALLENGE

Stand in front of a long mirror and do a top-to-toe check. Make a list of things that you may wish to do to enhance and present the "Best You" to the world. Don't be too critical or hard on yourself.

Next, on the same piece of paper, write a list about all the things you like about yourself. Don't be shy; no one has to see this list if you don't want them to! Search your heart for the beautiful things about you and write them down, then read it back to yourself – then write some more! Place no limit on this list, in fact the more on it the better.

By making subtle changes and emphasising your best points you will begin to realise how uniquely fabulous you really are.

Then you can really begin to show the world the 'Best You'!

Learn to laugh a lot

Develop a sense of humour if laughing doesn't come naturally – it is great for the soul.

Be able to laugh at yourself. This eliminates any pretentiousness and gives you a freedom to be you without making a harsh judgment of yourself. In addition, it keeps you humble! See the funny side of situations and have the ability to draw humour out of it when appropriate; this is a good quality which people appreciate. Laughter is infectious and people are drawn to people who laugh, they are a lot of fun to be with. (Girls, I don't mean loud squealing laughter.)

Keep things light, and foster a spirit of fun amongst people. Maintain a sense of humour in most circumstances. This will allow others in your company to feel relaxed and open towards you. Laughter breaks tension during difficult circumstances and puts people at ease.

A good sense of humour and an ability to laugh frequently at yourself helps us to keep life balanced and to enjoy most situations we find ourselves in. Laughter truly is one of the best medicines (it is scientifically proven!). Don't be afraid to be a little kooky or crazy at times, it can really be a lot of fun! Let go of pretence and let the child within out to play (now and again). Remember life is worth living and laughter is vital to our health and wellbeing.

Personal Comment:

My husband and I have learnt how to find the funny side of almost everything we come across these days.

It wasn't always this way with me; it's something I have had to work on. As a child I didn't have a lot to laugh about, so it wasn't a natural thing for me. I was sensitive and intense a lot of the time, was often told I didn't have a sense of humour, so believed it.

My husband has a great sense of humour and has helped me learn to laugh. We now laugh our way through our days while still working hard and accomplishing our goals. I personally know a sense of humour can be developed even if it's not a natural inclination.

I believe life really is fun and people really are funny. Don't miss it. The ability to laugh at yourself first really helps - there is a lot to laugh at when you look at yourself!

HEATHER SAYS
"LEARN TO LAUGH AS YOU GO!"

GIRLTALK CHALLENGE

Take note of how many times in your day you laugh, or even just giggle.

Start with having a giggle about yourself. Find something you do or say that is funny. We all have so many things about ourselves to laugh at (in a kind and loving way), so if we begin with ourselves, it helps our sense of humour and sense of fun develop.

Just take a moment to see the many things in each day to laugh at. Make a choice to 'Laugh A Lot' from now on!

Let your  speak

Your heart is the most beautiful part of you. It is the essence of who you are (your spirit).

- Listen carefully to what your heart is telling you.
- Your heart wants to speak – let it speak and listen to it.
- Your heart knows your true purpose.
- Your heart knows the truth.
- Give your heart permission to speak.
- Give your heart voice.
- Think about what makes your heart beat faster with excitement.
- Think about what makes your heart ache. What are you passionate about?
- When you speak from your heart you will open the hearts of others.

Nurture your heart, guard it and keep it safe.

"Above all else, guard your heart for it is the wellspring of life" **PROVERBS 4:23**[8]

PERSONAL COMMENT:

I believe letting your heart speak is a beautiful thing. There is no right or wrong when a heart speaks. It is what it is and it says what it says. Your true heart will speak the truth and it will be a defining moment for you. Sit up and take notice.

I believe your heart will say things to you your mind will not have thought about. Your heart will speak to you without pollution of distortion. Please, girlfriend, listen carefully to your heart.

When you allow your heart to speak, it will say the most beautiful things. It will speak the TRUTH to you.

HEATHER SAYS
"YOUR ♥ KNOWS THE TRUTH!"

GIRLTALK CHALLENGE

Find a quiet time with no distractions, somewhere warm and comfortable.

Be still and listen to your heart as it speaks to you. It will do so with love and gentleness.

It is a wonderfully profound experience.

I encourage you to do this. Listen to your beautiful heart.

Relationships

COMMUNICATION

Lines of communication as seen in the spirit

Healthy family relationships

We need to clearly identify and understand the different types of relationships we have within our families in order to keep each of these healthy. Being a loving woman does not mean you give in to the expectations and demands of others, nor compromise yourself in these relationships. Rather, you should enhance and be enhanced by these relationships – each relationship should contribute positively to the other.

Members of a healthy family will respect each other and support each other at all times, regardless of personality variations and differences of opinion.

Knowing how to manage family dynamics and how to bring something positive into each of the different relationships within the family can be extremely useful in creating a happy balance for you within the family. Understand the different responsibilities you have in each role and know how to respond with sensitivity in each situation, fulfilling your role with love and support.

Women play many roles in family relationships:

- Wife/partner
- Daughter
- Mother
- Granddaughter
- Grandmother
- Sister
- Daughter in law
- Mother in law
- Sister in law

Wife and Partner – This relationship needs to be be a loving, respectful and equal partnership, considering the other person at all times. I believe this relationship needs to have your 100% commitment and priority. This relationship can be the most beautiful and rewarding of all your relationships, if you play your part wisely. Understand the importance of valuing and protecting this relationship at all times, because so much of your life is affected by the success of this relationship. Taking care of it will reward you in many ways. The average bloke is a kind-hearted man who wants to be loved, respected and, very importantly, NEEDED! Men love to be needed by their wife/partner. This is very important at the core of who he is. Give him priority if you want this relationship to be successful.

Mother – As a mother, it's important you are open, warm and loving, so your family members know they can count on you no matter what happens. Be a disciplined woman who sets a good example for your children. Pour an unlimited amount of unconditional love onto your children, while at the same time setting clear guidelines for them. Be consistent in your parenting and teach your children to have values. Understand your responsibility and make it a priority in your life, so in turn your children will love and respect you. Be the person you want your children to become. Nothing can replace the unconditional love of a mother. If this is missing, a child will have trouble developing into a healthy, well balanced adult. The love of a mother is one of the most important aspects of human life. It is one thing to say you love your children, it is quite another to them to FEEL and SEE your love towards them. Obviously it is important to tell your children you love them on a regular basis, but love in action speaks volumes.

Daughter – As a daughter, love your parents dearly, be kind and helpful, holding your parents in high regard, honouring them for all they have done for you. Daughters can have a close, strong bond with their parents. Do your best to maintain a loving and healthy relationship with your parents. Have the ability to view this relationship with the long-term best interests of the family at heart. Be aware how much joy you can bring to your parents if you play your role well. As your parents get on in their years, ensure their comfort and security to the best of your ability. As a daughter, remember your parents gave you life.

Sometimes daughters carry a lot of responsibility in families and it can be difficult at times. Often the care of parents falls to the daughter. But stick with it, you are doing the right thing! Honouring your parents is a major part of a successful family and it speaks well for future generations.

Daughter in law – As daughter in law respect your in-laws; they are your husband/partner's parents. Support a close relationship between your husband/partner and his parents and put his best interests above your own in this relationship. Understand where you fit as a daughter in law and carry this role with respect and dignity. Remember your in-laws gave that gorgeous man of yours life, so they can't be that bad!

Grandmother - Love and spoil your grandchildren, spend lots of time with them (if possible) teaching and carefully guiding them, demonstrating good values and imparting wisdom from your experience. A grandmother can have a powerful and positive influence over her grandchildren's lives. You bring a significant and valuable addition to the parenting role, being careful not to undermine the parents but supporting them in the raising of your grandchildren. (This does not mean being a full time babysitter!) Enjoy your grandchildren. Make your time with them full of love and fun.

Granddaughter – Love your grandparents; include them in your life (if possible), respecting and learning from their wisdom and experience. Take time out to visit with them, if and when possible. Be grateful for having your grandparents in your life if you do - make the most of it! If you are unable to visit, send cards and letters, keeping them informed and included in your life. Don't underestimate the joy you bring as a grandchild. Make an effort; it will mean more than you will ever know and soon they will be gone. Do it while you can.

Sister - You and your siblings have an unspoken understanding, so extend a hand to them at all times. You encourage and cultivate a strong bond in these relationships. Do not make judgements on your brothers and sisters, but love them unconditionally. If you do this they will feel close to you and be there for you. Be careful not to judge - we all have different views. Give your siblings the freedom to live their lives without your judgement. They are your family – don't lose touch with them.

Sister in law – Respect and support your sibling's choice of partner. Be a friend to your sister in law; making her feel included as one of the family. Love your sister in law, she could be a good ally! It's never easy shaping up to a husband/partner's family. She may feel insecure with your family. Be her friend – she needs you.

Mother in law – This is a very important relationship requiring lots of love and support. Give encouragement and wait to be asked before giving advice. Hold your tongue and do not pass judgement. Respect your son/daughter's choice of partner and do all you can to help the couple without interfering in their personal matters. Wisdom is required to pull off this role successfully. The odds are stacked against us here. Often in this role we are damned if we do and damned if we don't. Respecting your child's choice should be priority. Remember your child (probably) loves this person. Less is better unless you are really sure. Love and respect will win at the end of the day.

Personal comment:

One of my favourite things to do is send beautiful cards to people, especially family members, to tell them how important they are to me.

I like to support the relationship by reminding the person in writing how much I value having them in my life.

Heather says
"We are family..."

IMPORTANT NOTE:

- It takes two willing people to have a successful relationship.
- Make sure you do your part with love, but know you are not responsible for the other person's response to you. For example, do not allow yourself to be mistreated or abused by someone just to stay in a relationship with them. A healthy relationship benefits all parties in a positive and good way.
- A loving, healthy relationship doesn't hurt.

GIRLTALK CHALLENGE

Consider each of the roles which apply to you.

Ask yourself what you can do to enhance this relationship.

Think of something kind and supportive to do and plan to do it.

Sometimes one kind gesture can go a long way.

Deposit something loving on a regular basis and watch it grow.

Relationships and maintaining them

Quality relationships will determine your success and wellbeing in life and are so fundamental to our basic needs as human beings - being loved and accepted without judgement, along with loving and accepting others without judgement.

Placing people in their right place in your life is the key to maintaining good relationships. Allowing people to step into areas of your life they should not be in will inevitably cause relationship problems. Clear boundaries are required for healthy long-term relationships. Relationships worth holding onto take time and effort. You get out of relationships what you put into them. If you put love and support into a relationship, you will get love and support from it. Equally, if you put criticism and judgement into a relationship, you will get criticism and judgement from it.

- Understand not all people should take an equal place in your life; some deserve a larger place and some a smaller place, depending on the circumstances and type of relationship. Not everyone you meet is supposed to be your friend and have a place in your life. Not everyone who is part of your life should be very close to you.

Sometimes it is time to close the door on certain relationships as you move through your life – and that is okay! This can make room for the right people, for the next season on your journey. Be careful not to get tied to people who won't let you go with dignity and respect. This may be people who are clingy, or emotionally dependent on you.

Examples:

- Family: obviously these people are at the top of your list and should hold a place of priority.
- Friendships: important but should not override family.
- Professional: important too, but keep them in perspective with your time and priority. Make sure these relationships really are a benefit to you professionally. It is easy to get sidetracked with these relationships and to blur the line between professional and social.
- Social acquaintances: these relationships should be only occasional if you are to keep the right balance in your life.
- Female: female relationships are great, but make sure you understand where each one fits and give it the appropriate place and time. Not all relationships are equal and not all relationships are good for you.
- Male: male relationships take more management and consideration to keep them in their right place, and keeping the relationship to what's appropriate. Platonic male/female relationships need very clear boundaries around them e.g. a friendly relationship with your girlfriend's husband. Careful! Careful!

Women need to understand familiarity; control and manipulation are not part of healthy relationships and these things arise out of the lack of healthy boundaries.

Many women get caught up in controlling and manipulating behaviour without realising it. It's important to be honest with yourself on this issue. This behaviour is unhealthy and unattractive and will always create dissatisfaction in relationships. It will most often end in relationships being destroyed and people being hurt. Many women fall into this type of behaviour out of fear and insecurity.

Guard against being too busy to invest time into valuable and appropriate relationships that are important not only now, but later in life.

Personal Comment:

Honestly, sometimes I feel tired just saying the word 'relationship', but the reality is quality relationships take time and energy. Actually, I sometimes find keeping close relationships healthy, balanced and rewarding exhausting, but life is all about relationships, connections and interaction with others. So it's important to be disciplined and careful in our relationships, because I have found when they go wrong, it is very painful and takes a lot more energy to repair them.

Relationships are the most beautiful thing in the world and in our lives. I am still learning how to do them better each day! I know being whole spiritually, mentally and emotionally is my personal responsibility. When people take something broken into a relationship, chances are they will cause damage and hurt others. Healing yourself first will help you have beautiful relationships and maintain them long-term. Quality, loving relationships are rewarding and will bring you much joy.

I have learnt my husband and my family need to get the majority of my space and time (within reason) and other friends and acquaintances, colleagues all get more calculated space and time. Again, it's all about balance. I have learnt to be wise with my spaces and whom I let into them.

Heather says
"We are personally responsible for our relationships"

GIRLTALK CHALLENGE

Choose one relationship you have at the present that is very important to you, a person you want to be in a close, respectful relationship for a lifetime.

Decide what YOU are going to put into that relationship to deepen and maintain it, so it has an opportunity to be all you hope it will be.

Realise it's your responsibility to look after that relationship. Nurture it so it will be good to you.

Effective communication

Communicating effectively with people is another key to a successful and rewarding life.

- Effective communication is a learned art.
- Even people who are born talkers are not necessarily effective communicators.
- Effective communication includes listening and engaging with others.
- Listening carefully to what others are saying helps you communicate more effectively.
- Don't be in too much of a hurry to have your say.
- We can learn so much from others by respectfully listening. Sometimes, if we take the time, we will learn from the people we least expect to. There is an art to listening effectively.
- Be careful not to dismiss people. Most people have something to offer you or teach you, if you allow them to.
- Using people's names during communication helps to personalise discussion. This makes others feel important and shows you are sincerely interested and respect them.
- Asking about people's families is a good way to initiate a conversation or to bridge a conversation.
- Make sure you know the news of the day or current topics. This also helps in conversation with strangers.
- Effective communicators know it's NOT all about them.
- Don't be afraid to confront with honesty and integrity. Bring solutions to problems when dealing with issues.
- Understand the power of your words in the lives of others.
- Have discernment in recognising a delicate situation and tread carefully and sensitively.
- It is better to remove yourself politely than to stay in a discussion which is rapidly deteriorating and will not produce anything positive at that time.

- Don't talk down to others or make them feel inadequate or intimidated.
- A good tip is if in doubt, leave it out – don't say it.
- Effective communicators help others to express themselves.
- Don't try to impress people with big fancy words you know they don't understand; you will risk looking rather foolish yourself.
- Don't dominate conversation; allow others to have their say and feel part of the discussion.
- An equal exchange is when both parties have had the opportunity to talk and listen, with something valuable being imparted and received.
- Effective communicators end discussion by clarifying any important points raised to avoid any misunderstandings.
- At the end, be sure to leave the way open for further contact (if that is desired).
- The professional gap is vital for communication in the work place.
- Timing is important in successful communication.
- Do not go into a meeting or situation unprepared. Do not try to 'wing it' – everyone will know.
- Always finish on a positive note, and leave doors open.

It's a small world. You just never know.

Personal Comment:

I admit I can be a bit of a talker. I have to be mindful of listening to others – I get bored very quickly if the communication is not moving fast and getting to the point. I love fast-moving discussion which is challenging and productive. I know I can be seen as rude when I try to hurry the conversation along so this is something I am working on.

However, I believe I should be careful of who I engage in communication with, so I don't put myself or others in unpleasant situations. It is a fine line to walk because at the same time I don't want to be considered aloof or superior.

Professional communication needs slightly different consideration than personal communication. I try to have a good balance between talking and listening in every situation, but when I am passionate about something it can be difficult to shut me up. My darling husband will testify to that.

I don't profess to be an expert, because I am not. However, with 30 years in businesses where communication and dealing with large numbers of people was the key part of my role, I learnt some things along the way. Sure, I made a lot of mistakes, but I also learnt valuable lessons.

Gifted communicators are a joy to listen to. (Just because someone talks a lot doesn't mean they are gifted communicators.) I agree with the phrase it's not how much people say, it's what they say, what they impart that is positive and life changing. I also believe silence, used appropriately, can be a beautiful form of communication. A certain 'look' or a smile can be the perfect form of communication at times.

Try "You talk and I will listen" – you may be surprised at what you hear. I have been.

HEATHER SAYS
"COMMUNICATE EFFECTIVELY AND CONNECT"

GIRLTALK CHALLENGE

Spend some time with a close friend and just listen.

If you need to, ask questions to get the conversation started, but make a point of listening for at least 70% of the time you spend together.

You may discover something amazing you never knew about your friend.

"I have come to believe...that what is most important to me must be spoken, made verbal and shared, even at the risk of having it bruised or misunderstood." **AUDRE LORDE**[13]

It's just 'no'

It is important to know when to say NO, yet women often have difficulty saying NO. It doesn't come naturally for many of us as mothers, wives, partners, friends or work colleagues because some of us have become people pleasers and lost our ability to say NO to things that are not appropriate for us, and to things that are not our responsibility. We seem to have lost the ability to recognise what belongs to us and what does not.

No can be a very positive word, when you are refusing to accept something that is not the best for you and indeed for others you are responsible for. No is a protective boundary word. The word no protects us from what we know is not right. If we learn to use this word at the right time, it can save us from a lot of unpleasantness and unnecessary stress, and much worse.

There are many things in society today and in our relationships to which we should be saying no for ourselves and for our families. We have lowered our standards considerably in recent times with an "anything goes" and "everything is acceptable" attitude.

By doing this we have opened ourselves up to much harm without fully understanding what we have done. There is a consequence to all of our actions and we need to be very careful before readily accepting things we know are not right, or even things we are unsure of. It's so easy to be deceived by media, peer pressure, manipulative people, wanting to please others etc.

If we are to be women who clearly discern right from wrong, what is harmful, what will have negative consequences, then no will be a word we are confident using, and we will use it more frequently than we have in the past. Unfortunately there are many more things we need to be saying no to if we want to live life well. Remember the choice is ours. It may be difficult at times but removing things from your life that are causing problems can only be a positive thing, surely.

If saying no brings you peace, gives you freedom to make your own decisions that are right for you and removes inappropriate things from your life, then learning to say no at the right time, for the right reason is a key factor to living a life you are in control of and enjoying.

When saying no you do not have to add excuses or give explanations; you have the right to just say no. Learn to say no politely and graciously – for example "Thank you so much for asking me but no thank you".

Personal Comment:

Based on my own experience and learning, I believe most of us have trouble saying no, because we don't want to be seen as uncooperative or difficult. We need to be firm in our values, know our worth and say NO and feel okay about it, not guilty. Knowing when to say NO will then become very clear to you and you will feel right about it because you have maintained your standard.

I admit it took me years to 'get this'. I was a people-pleaser. I didn't want to let anyone down. Needless to say, I was doing almost everything for everyone else and neglecting my own priorities. I certainly don't do this now and it feels good to be free of that.

I understand no is my friend. My friend no has given me the ability to pursue new and interesting avenues which have added richness and value to my life and the lives of those around me.

HEATHER SAYS
"NO IS MY FRIEND AND MY PROTECTOR"

GIRLTALK CHALLENGE

Is there something in your diary, or on your schedule, that you absolutely do not want to take part in and have been dreading?

Then I suggest you make a decision immediately to communicate that to the appropriate person or people.

Remember it is your right to say NO (politely).

Notice how it feels once you have done it.

HUMILITY

The Humble Black Swan lowers his head

Consideration for others

Consideration for others is thinking things through from the perspective of others; considering the facts at hand. It is important for women to know how to address issues in our lives without causing mayhem, offending or hurting others.

- Choose carefully the time and place to address issues with people. Keep an open mind, consider the point of view of others. Listening carefully is important when dealing with sensitive issues. Don't do this at a time when you are angry and upset, or the other person or people may be upset.
- Wait until you are in control and not overly emotional, so you have a balanced view and are able to consider their position as well as your own.
- Showing consideration to others is very empowering and most people will respect and respond to you favourably when you do this.
- Openly show consideration for others. This opens people's minds to receive what you are saying or proposing.
- Make consideration for others a high priority in all you do. You will get their support and respect when they realise they are a priority to you.
- Make it clear you are considering others in your decision-making or viewpoints.

Please note: Consideration of others is not compromising your values. Make sure you fully understand the difference. Considering others does not necessarily mean changing your plan or view just to keep others happy. It's taking time to consider others, their positions and their feelings and will help you reduce the risk of people becoming upset and offence being caused.

Discerning the needs of others

Take notice when others are in need; allow yourself to recognise when someone else requires help or maybe a kind word. Ask yourself whether you are sensitive to other people's needs when you're in their company. It is not difficult to notice whether those around you are in need when you are sincerely concerned for others.

Helping others is one of the most important aspects of our lives. It is more blessed to give than receive. If we don't do this, we miss out on life's most rewarding experiences. Actually I believe we were not put on this earth for ourselves, so we miss our true purpose if we do not attend to the needs of others. The key is to not be so consumed with yourself and your own problems, you do not notice when someone in your presence is hurting or struggling. Helping others, even when you have concerns of your own, is often your best cure for your own problems.

Tune in to the needs of others; put others first. Who knows, they may just have the answer to your problem! Be considerate – that is why you are here and whatever situation you find yourself in, it's always about helping others.

You may be thinking "When am I going to have time for this?" but it doesn't necessarily have to be something big or time consuming. Little things for others every day go a long way. It's like the ripple effect – a drop in the ocean has an effect that travels far.

Sometimes people just want to know you have considered and thought of them in a situation that will affect them. If you want to keep your relationships healthy, consideration of others is a must. Letting them know you have thought of them is often enough to make them feel valued; then they are more likely to understand your point of view or your position.

If we live our lives not recognising and attending to the needs of those around us, we miss the whole purpose of our own life. It really is time for us to stop being selfish. For most of us, we live a very nice life, thank you very much. We don't need to spend 100% of our time on ourselves. God has given us enough time for ourselves and lots of other people too. So let's get to it and start to invest our time and consideration in others.

Personal Comment:

I have discovered service to others above my own need is really where the best life is. Once you begin to understand this, your own selfish needs diminish in your own eyes and the needs of others begin to consume you. You will find yourself on a journey of pursuing the needs of others everywhere you go. In my pursuit of happiness, I have found it in meeting the needs of others in any way I am able to. Service above self is the key to true happiness.

"Not everyone can be famous, but everyone can be great, because greatness is determined by service." **MARTIN LUTHER KING**[14]

Heather says
"It's not only about you"

GIRLTALK CHALLENGE

In the next few days I challenge you to take notice and consider carefully the needs of others in your daily walk - in your home, family and work place.

Take a few moments to notice whether there is anyone in your environment who may need some help, consideration and encouragement.

A kind word, some time, a listening ear, a hug – someone might need to know someone cares.

Men and women together

Be secure in who you are as a person and as a woman. Position yourself confidently in this place so you can view men with value and respect and don't feel you have to change them or feel threatened by them.

Men and women operate differently. Understand and value it, realising most men who are honoured and respected give the same in return to women. (Note I said most, not all!) Know the role a man fits into and allow him to excel in that role, without putting unrealistic expectations on him. Free him to do the things he is designed for and the things he does best!

I have found most men will do almost anything to help women when they are treated with appreciation and respect. Come on girls, let's get smart. Men want to feel needed, not bullied and controlled. Controlling the men in our life to make them into what we want them to be is not valuing and respecting them. This is an area some women need to closely look at. Men are a wonderful gift to us and vice versa; let's get with the programme.

Bossy, aggressive, unappreciative behaviour towards men is not only unattractive, it produces nothing positive. We need to develop the skills to handle these relationships in a way that give both parties value, respect and dignity.

Women don't need to be like men, they should be who they are - a woman - and let men be who they are – a man. Often women sabotage their relationships with men and then blame the man for the problem, because they do not understand the differences between the genders.

Men should be allowed to voice their opinions and women should listen without judging or criticising, or worse, verbally attacking. Maybe we need to think about how we would cope with being verbally attacked, the way some of us are to our men. (Please note 'some of us' – not all.)

We need to value our men much more and give them the opportunity to be all we want them to be without control or manipulation. Don't bombard men with talking and raving; plan carefully when you need to communicate something of concern to them. When men get bombarded, they switch off and retreat. Give them space when they need to digest what you have said to them. Don't keep going on at them; they are unable to handle this kind of behaviour. If you give them respect and time then most men will respond. (Note, I said most men.)

A loving, respectful, calm, peaceful relationship with a man is one of the most beautiful things in life. Let's learn how to do this well, so we don't miss out on what they have to offer us.

Let's work together, not against each other

Now we understand the differences, let's talk about bringing the differences together. Know that by working together with men and using the talents and strengths of both male and female, the outcome is more balanced and more effective. Understanding the relational and factual dynamics of both male and female, then joining these forces in a positive way can prove to be an unbeatable combination. Partnerships working correctly are very creative and powerful.

Do not threaten men, but draw out the strengths in them to enhance what we as women do not possess. To make the partnership work to its fullest potential, allow both parties to do what they do best in combination. Realise men and women are truly two halves which make a whole when the relationship (personal or professional) is operating effectively and healthily.

Women have enormous untapped potential, but when partnered with men, can release something amazing for both parties. In some cases it takes partnering with men for the women's potential to surface and vice versa. Don't miss out on this. It's another of life's incredible experiences.

Men and women communicate very differently. Women like to talk everything over and over. Men do not. We need to learn how to communicate effectively with our men so they don't shut down on us. There are lots of good books on this subject. If you have never read one you really need to as soon as possible. Once you understand it, it changes so much in our relationships with the wonderful male species.

'Men are from Mars, Women are from Venus' by Dr John Gray[15] is a helpful book to read. Women need to understand it's important not to compete with men. Men bring a valuable and necessary contribution to most situations if we are to have balance.

We need to give our men a chance to prove their worth. So often we dismiss them, because they think differently. Of course they think differently, they are men! Let's not be prideful and foolish girls – embrace men with love and respect and they may surprise and delight us.

66

PERSONAL COMMENT:

I have discovered on my journey in relationships with men that they love to be needed; they need to feel and be told they have value. As women today we are very independent and capable. This can make men feel they have no place. Although girls we are extremely capable on our own, when we do things together with men, a dynamic synergy can take place that is unique to the woman/man combination.

HEATHER SAYS
"GIVE OUR MEN A FAIR GO"

99

GIRLTALK CHALLENGE

Whatever your age, if you have never read some of the books on the differences between men and women, do not delay.

The knowledge will change your life and add a new appreciation for the gorgeous men in your life.

Make it a priority to inform yourself on the wonderful differences between men and women.

Great friendships

- Great friendships are another one of life's great pleasures. Life is about people, yes really!
- Great friends are considerate, understanding and very loyal to the people they care about.
- Great friends understand true friendships are based on unconditional love and support for one another. They know criticism and judgement do not belong in true friendships.
- Great friends are disciplined in communication. They are careful not to fall into gossip, which they know only brings hurt to others and has the potential to destroy friendships.
- True friendship always offers a helping hand while supporting the dreams and aspirations of others.
- True friends are there in the good and bad times.
- Friends forgive each other – they know they themselves are not perfect and in need of forgiveness also.
- True friendship values the differences in people and appreciates them.

True friendship does not become jealous, but is happy for the good fortune of others.

Value friendships and make time in your busy lives to nurture them; fostering great friendships takes time and consideration. A small but sincere group of friends you can trust is far better than many acquaintances.

Women often let themselves down in the area of trust. Breaking confidences is something women need to be careful not to do. True great friends are 100% trustworthy.

What Kind of Girlfriend are You?

I encourage you to step into the role of a Great Girlfriend – you will then be rare and precious, with high value to those fortunate enough to have you in their lives.

A Great Girlfriend...

- would speak well of me at all times and not gossip or criticise me. She would have a disciplined tongue, even when she might be tempted to fall into saying something she knows she shouldn't.
- would be quick to forgive me if I offend or hurt her. She would understand people sometimes do or say things unintentionally or without being sensitive to others. None of us is perfect.
- would see the good things in me and not focus on my weaknesses and faults. This is what keeps our friendship alive and on a mature level.
- would stand by me in the tough times as well as the good times. She would be prepared to get into the trenches and do battle alongside me, as well as celebrating with me.
- would be 100% trustworthy in all things and would not break confidences. She understands breaking confidences will destroy the friendship. Breaking a confidence will also break your girlfriend's heart.
- would be genuinely pleased when things go well for me and not be jealous or envious. She does not compare her life with mine; she is secure in herself and in her own life.
- would support me in my dreams for my life. She would encourage me to keep believing in my dreams and working towards them.
- would be sensitive to my needs and be a good listener. She knows I don't want her advice unless I ask for it, because friendship is as much about listening as it is about talking.
- would love and appreciate the differences between us and not try to change me. She would celebrate our differences, recognising we each have something different to offer and what a blessing this is to our friendship.
- would be my cheerleader. She would at every opportunity cheer me on, even when others may have stopped. I know I can always rely on her to be there for me.

Great girlfriends are indeed hard to find, but the rewards of being a truly trustworthy, loving friend are enormous. Don't forget what we sow, we reap. I encourage you to sow well into your close girlfriends.

Personal Comment:

After many years of being too busy with my career and family to foster friendships, I now realise this was unbalanced and I robbed myself of one of life's greatest pleasures – being with true friends. I am pleased to say in the past few years I have corrected this situation and now have a group of amazing friends whose love and support for me is humbling indeed. I value each and every one highly. They are all different but equally brilliant.

On the other side of the coin, there have been a few occasions when I have discovered girlfriends I believed were true friends and valued me as I valued them were not true friends at all. I'd like to share one tough lesson – you may even be wrestling with something similar yourself.

A girlfriend frequently made little remarks about me in front of others, sometimes in a joking way, but it always left me with a yucky feeling inside. After spending time with her, rather than feeling uplifted and encouraged, I would go away uneasy, with a nervy feeling in the pit of my stomach. I later discovered through a true and trusted friend the other woman had been criticising me, making judgements about me. She had also been undermining me to my family and friends, causing them to doubt me. I was deeply hurt. I eventually confronted her about it. She denied having meant any harm but I was relieved to be upfront and face to face. I removed myself from her circle and stopped contact with her and the situation improved all round.

I want to have a bunch of Great Girlfriends to grow old with, so we can reminisce and drink coffee and laugh together. I am building those friendships now for future reward.

Heather says
"Different, but equally brilliant"

GIRLTALK CHALLENGE

Be the Great Girlfriend to others you want to have yourself.

Make sure you give your girlfriends whatever you want from them - loyalty, love, forgiveness, time and support. You will then be blessed in return.

This week do something with or for a valued girlfriend that would have her see you as important in her life.

Network with like-minded people

It's enjoyable to be with all kinds of women with different interests, personalities and skills. However, it's important to link with like-minded women for support and encouragement, to gain fresh ideas and to be inspired by one another.

- People play an important part in your life by helping you to progress. Everyone we choose to have in our life, will help us or hinder our journey. Choose carefully.
- We are all here to learn something from other people and to teach something to others.
- It is important to know who you're teaching and who you are learning from.
- Giving to and receiving from others is an important balance in living life well.
- Delete relationships which hold you back or undermine you. Everyone we meet or know isn't necessarily meant to be part of our life, contrary to some beliefs. Wrong relationships can be very destructive.
- Network with women who have similar interests and mindsets. They will stretch and pull you into new things.
- Women who are further on in the journey than you can be marvellous mentors.

Being with like-minded people is the key to networking productively. Don't network for the sake of it, to be seen or appear popular. Be strategic in your networking; it takes time and effort. A good networking relationship works both ways - giving and receiving equation is win/win.

Stay in regular contact with people of like minds, who stimulate you, challenge your thinking, encourage you and extend you to go further; people who leave you feeling inspired and feeling good about who you are.

Personal Comment:

I have found networking with like-minded women keeps me sharp and stretches me into new things. I love to hear what successful women think and how they achieve their goals. I am fairly competitive by nature, so networking with successful women motivates me. I very much enjoy meeting someone and begin talking, to find a moment of connection where I know the person has something wonderful and valuable to teach me. Being open to learning always brings me something new.

Heather says
"Network and learn"

Girltalk Challenge

Seek out someone who is on a similar path to you, but further along the journey.

Someone you admire, someone who inspires you.

Get alongside her and begin to network in the same circles.

Freedom without judgement

- Judgement can be a harsh, cruel expression which hurts, hinders and destroys.
- Allow those around you the freedom to be themselves without criticism.
- It is not your place to make judgement on other people's lives.
- It is unhealthy to place judgement on others when we ourselves are not perfect.
- It's better to focus on keeping our own lives in order.

Placing judgement on others can be very harmful, to them and to yourself. It ties you to circumstances to which you do not belong. Do not get involved where you are not meant to be. Learn to keep your opinions to yourself unless asked.

This is a trap women often fall into. Having opinions and expressing views about others is none of your business and out of order. We need to have a disciplined tongue. Remember, what you sow you reap. Keep relationships free from judgement. This will make healthier relationships and give them a better chance of being long-term and rewarding. Most people know when you are making harsh judgements on them; they can sense it even if they don't hear it.

PERSONAL COMMENT:

It seems to me to be part of our inherent nature to judge others without understanding or knowing the facts. It grieves me to hear people place judgement on others, while expecting none on themselves. I urge you to get to the point where you understand it is really none of your business (most of the time); it's a very freeing experience. Move on to more positive and productive things.

I notice women often feel the need to express opinion and judgement on others. I have discovered the person who is continually judging and criticising is often a person who is hurting over something that has happened to her and her view of life in general is quite negative.

Of course, I realise we're all human and will judge from time to time. When I find myself doing this, I stop it and ask God to forgive me and to release me from the situation I have just placed judgement on.

"Do not judge, or you too will be judged. For in the same way you judge others, you will be judged, and with the measure you use, it will be measured to you" **MATTHEW 7:1**

HEATHER SAYS
"MIND YOUR OWN BUSINESS"

GIRLTALK CHALLENGE

In the next few days, listen carefully to discussions going on around you.

Identify negative judgement being voiced.

This will help you identify when you yourself fall into this trap.

The team dynamic

The ability of people to work together in unity with each other and for each other is a rare gift. People who serve each other in a team dynamic allow the team to produce something far greater than the individuals could. Serving the bigger purpose produces bigger results.

The talents and gifts of individuals can be enhanced in a team environment when the right people are placed together and work as a team. When they give their own talents and gifts, then combine them with the gifts and talents of others, what is created will be bold, big and beautiful. A team of people, such as family, workplace or sports team, working together for each other can become an unbeatable force.

Aim to always have the team view, not an individualistic one. Become a visionary who sees the bigger picture. People committed to the team understand the power of the team and are not interested in self service. People talk a lot about the team but I personally have rarely seen it in action working as well as I believe it can. Where there is absolute UNITY, the supernatural can happen and often does. A saying I have recalled and repeated over many years is "One ox can pull two tonnes, but two oxen harnessed together and walking in unison can pull 20 tonnes."

"Where there is unity there is a blessing." **PSALM 133**[6]

PERSONAL COMMENT:

I believe none of us was intended to work alone or live alone. I know people need people and need relationships with each other to survive healthily. I believe most people need the talents and gifts of others to enhance their own.

I have observed individual egos often stand in the way of the dynamic ability of the team. Some people would rather have a little glory themselves than have the phenomenal result of a team and share it with others. I believe the ultimate big picture team result should be our desire, but our egos need dealing with for this to occur. I know we girls are good at working as a team when we stop competing, to understand we all have equal value in what we bring to the team.

Individually, we do not possess all the qualities, talents and experience required to achieve great results. My experience has been unity and cohesion produce results which individuals cannot. I personally like drawing on the talent of the team – we can all grow and learn from others. Together is better and a lot more fun.

HEATHER SAYS
"TOGETHER IS ALWAYS BETTER"

GIRLTALK CHALLENGE

Challenge yourself to begin thinking as 'We' and not 'I'.

'We' as in workplace, home, family, friends, sport etc.

'We' can achieve more than 'I'.

Quick to apologise

We all make mistakes. A mistake won't define you, but what you do after it might.

Be honest when you make a mistake. You are not a failure because you make the odd mistake. A woman who is quick to take responsibility and apologise when she makes a mistake is a person of maturity, integrity and humility.

Don't be afraid to freely admit when you are wrong. To quickly apologise takes a strong sense of who you are and displays excellent character. It makes a powerful statement to others, and is an example that others follow. It is also very liberating for you and for those around you – a heartfelt apology releases you from the situation to move on and leads the way for others to do the same.

Be sincere with your apologies, so those who receive them will know you mean it. They will be quick to accept your apology, happy to move on and not hold a grudge. A sincere apology has a humbling quality that illuminates a high level of maturity and security in oneself. Apologising is also very empowering. It leaves you in a strong position to go forward.

If you are not sincere, your apology will be meaningless.

PERSONAL COMMENT:

I personally find it very easy to apologise these days, even when I am not sure I need to. I notice it stops anything negative and destructive from creeping into the situation.

But most of all it keeps my soul well. I don't always 'feel' like it, but I have come to know an apology will usually bring a useful result.

I don't let pride stop me from apologising – it is amazing how good I feel after I have said the word 'Sorry'. I don't mean I always admit I was wrong if I really believe I wasn't but apologising for causing others upset, hurt or confusion solves many a problem before it escalates into something greater.

To apologise is also a sign of humility - which is one of the most beautiful qualities a person can have.

HEATHER SAYS
"KEEP A HUMBLE HEART"

GIRLTALK CHALLENGE

Apologise to someone today if you think you have hurt or upset them.

You don't have to admit you were wrong if you don't believe you were, but apologise for a situation where trust or a relationship has been damaged e.g. "You know when such and such happened, I am sorry if I caused you any upset, hurt or inconvenience."

Forgiveness
on your sleeve

We have all hurt people in the past and will probably still do so in the future, because we are human and our human nature has many flaws. It's important we understand this, take responsibility for it and be more aware of it.

Even when we may not intend to hurt others, it sometimes happens through no fault of our own, because it largely depends on where the other person is in their life and the way they perceive things. So forgiveness needs to play a significant role in our lives - whether it is forgiving others who hurt us or asking someone to forgive you. Giving and receiving forgiveness are equally important. When you understand this fully, it helps you stay free and moving on with your life.

Forgiveness is a choice, not a feeling. We seldom feel like forgiving, particularly if we are angry and hurt, but we can choose to do so. Be wise and forgive someone today and set yourself free from the prison of resentment and bitterness. Resentment will keep you from the best in life and will keep you in the position of victim and in a life of pain.

- Have the strength and courage to choose to forgive those who hurt you, in order to move on and not let unpleasant experiences keep you from the best life has to offer you. Understand forgiveness plays an important part in keeping you healthy and well. Forgiveness is about you and for you.
- Pride is never helpful in these situations; in fact your own pride and bitterness can be worse than the offence. Forgiveness truly frees you from the situation.

- Forgiveness is a major key to living a great life. It helps to keep you free from carrying around 'baggage'.
- Forgiveness can be a difficult choice to make when you are hurting, but do it for yourself, set yourself free from the offence and don't allow a victim mentality to get established within you. Not forgiving can affect your health and well being. It can distort your view of your world and the people in it.
- Forgiveness is a choice, so start with verbalising the forgiveness statement and say it as many times as you need to in order to begin to feel a change in your feelings and in your heart, to feel your power return to you.

> The Forgiveness Statement: 'I forgive _____ and I release them from my judgement. I set myself free and the person who hurt me free so we both move on to better things'.

- Forgiveness and Reconciliation are two separate processes: Forgiveness takes ONE, Reconciliation takes TWO.

Reconciliation is not always appropriate, but forgiveness is necessary to free yourself and move on.

> "Forgive us our trespasses as we forgive those who trespass against us" THE LORD'S PRAYER[6]

Personal Comment:

I have found forgiveness to be a process, but have made a conscious decision to forgive - if not for others, most certainly for myself. Forgiveness releases me from the situation that caused me pain. I believe I must always forgive those who hurt or abuse me. However, this does not mean I excuse or accept the behaviour, nor does it mean I have to be reconciled with that person.

For example: A man beats his wife. The wife needs to forgive the man so SHE can move on. But she need not accept what he did, nor have to be reconciled with him - especially if he has not had treatment or counselling.

I named this topic 'Forgiveness on Your Sleeve' because a number of years ago, after having a very hurtful thing happen to me, I found myself obsessed by the offence. I just couldn't get past it, so I developed a strategy to carry forgiveness on my sleeve (so to speak) so every time I thought about the situation and got hurt and just plain angry, I repeated the "Forgiveness Statement".

In the beginning I was saying this many times a day, but gradually realised I wasn't thinking about the situation nearly as much, and if I did it didn't hurt me or make me angry as it previously did. Then, one day I realised I hadn't thought about it for some time and it didn't affect me any more. I realised I had truly forgiven and moved on – and was free of the person and the hurt. Hallelujah!

Now I carry forgiveness on my sleeve everywhere I go because occasionally I still get hurt or offended by people – but I forgive them quickly and move on quickly.

Heather says
"Forgive and be free"

GIRLTALK CHALLENGE

Is there someone you are still angry with for the way they
have treated you?

If so, give the 'Forgiveness Statement' a go. Be sincere
and say it from your heart. Keep saying it until you feel a
change taking place.

It may take some time to feel the change, but take the
time to work towards it. I personally recommend it and
know it works.

Be a role model

- Be mindful people in your life may be influenced by you and make sure you conduct yourself as a positive role model.
- Realise you have a responsibility to everyone in your area of influence, but in particular to young people who will be looking up to you and perhaps attempting to mirror you. This applies particularly to your family.
- Don't underestimate your influence on others and aim to leave a positive lasting impression wherever possible.
- Understand your every word and action can enhance the lives of others around you if you choose to be a good role model at all times.
- Develop an acute awareness of others in your space and of your own conduct.
- Be consistent with your values and beliefs so people know you are a person they can rely on - having trust and confidence in you to remain the same.
- Ensure the behaviour you are modelling is behaviour you would be proud to see repeated in others. This principle applies no matter what age you are – however, as you get older, you certainly need to be considering this more carefully.

I believe parenting is probably one of, if not THE, most important role modelling we do. I urge you to consider a parenting course if you would like some fresh insight. After all, no one has really taught us how to parent – we all watch our own parents, so if your parents are good role models, you are fortunate.

Most of us learn to parent as we go and by our mistakes, so I encourage you to get good parenting advice, particularly for teenagers! Try to start when they are young to build a healthy relationship with your children, so the communication lines stay open.

Personal Comment:

I am continually surprised at how much of an influence on others we can be. It's a real reality check when I hear others around me behaving and speaking like me. When this happens, I am reminded of my responsibility to conduct myself well at all times, especially in the presence of others.

I was a parent to three teenagers and it was probably one of the most difficult times of my life. I spent much of my time during those years worrying and fretting about them. I read several books on the subject, but, looking back I think I should have gone to courses on parenting teenagers. Thank goodness I am through that time now and we all survived – Thank the Lord.

Heather says
"Be a good role model"

GIRLTALK CHALLENGE

Know whatever your age, you are a role model right now to someone in your life. Identify that person/persons and begin to examine whether you are setting a good example for them to follow.

Remember this includes what you say, what you do, how you take care of yourself, how you treat others etc.

Consider how to be a positive role model to someone in your life - they may be depending on you.

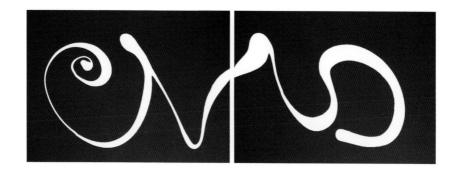

TWO ARE BETTER THAN ONE
The beauty of the pair!

Express yourself beautifully

Think back to the last time you received a caring expression from someone you know. Think how it felt to know that person cared enough to express his or her thoughts. Consider how you might leave that impression on someone you care about.

Put pen to paper, or finger to keyboard to express yourself to others and do it frequently.

- A note here and there, just to let someone know you care
- A few words in a card, a word of support
- A letter of encouragement, words of inspiration
- A word of thanks
- A journal of reflection
- A diary of record
- An uplifting word and encouragement to assist health and wellbeing

Know the beauty in the written word expressed in a way to lift the spirits of others.

Give creative licence to your soul. Let your soul dance with beautiful written words and express yourself through beautifully written words to open the heart of the reader. Encouraging, uplifting, edifying, loving, kind, sincere written words can change someone's life forever.

Go on, try it! Get yourself a journal and just write whatever comes to mind. Don't judge yourself, just write. It's also a good healing tool for people unable to voice certain things. Allow yourself the gift of expressing yourself with the written word, even if just for your own eyes.

Write something beautiful for someone today.

PERSONAL COMMENT:

I love the smooth flow of an ink pen gliding across paper and bringing life as it goes. I love the written word. I love poetry (the soulful kind), words dancing on the paper they are written on. Writing beautiful words makes my soul sing and dance. It is also another way to keep my heart open and expressive. It helps me to search my heart for the truth of who I am and what I have deep within me.

Years ago, on a long flight, I began to express my heart in words to the people I love the most in the world. I can tell you I surprised myself at what was released from deep within as I wrote. When those I had written to read my words, it added a deep richness to each of those relationships. It is still evident today.

HEATHER SAYS
"BEAUTIFUL WORDS WILL OPEN THE HEART
OF THE ONE WHO READS THEM"

GIRLTALK CHALLENGE

Take some time to send a gift of the written word from your heart to people you love.

Tell them what they mean to you. It will change you both in the most wonderful way.

Send a card, an e-mail, a text, a letter. I personally suggest a card or letter as it is fabulous to get something in the post and have to open it.

You can also have it as a keepsake to look back on and read from time to time.

EXPRESSION WITHOUT JUDGEMENT

Just let yourself go

The trust factor

Trust or lack of trust is the one thing that can change every and any circumstance in a moment. Trust is of paramount importance to us all from the moment we are born, until the moment we die. It operates on more levels than we can count and without it we live with doubt, confusion, insecurity, fear, suspicion and anxiety.

When trust is not established, or broken, I believe the true potential of the situation is lost. People cannot operate at their best when trust is absent, so I believe the level at which a person can give or perform directly relates to their level of trust. When trust is present, energy and focus go into the best possible outcome for all. Trust puts positive energy into a situation to create something – something productive, something lovely, something healthy, something magnificent.

Establishing trust takes time, commitment and honest communication. Clear guidelines for everyone to understand and follow are essential. It is important to take the time and make the effort to establish a strong trust base, particularly before embarking on something new, for example a relationship, a marriage, a business, a project. If trust is not clearly established at the beginning (it is difficult to go back and establish trust after the fact) or if it is broken, it is difficult to repair and in some cases it is not possible to repair.

Trust needs to be established and continually built upon. Trust moves regularly, depending on circumstances and people. Keep your eye on it and do what is necessary to protect it.

PERSONAL COMMENT:

Trust does not come easily for me. People I have trusted have let me down, as I am sure is the case for many people, but I have come to understand it's not about whether I should trust people or not, it's more about taking the time to establish a strong trust base in my relationships (personal and professional). Open and honest communication about the expectation begins to do this.

I have found the more honest I am about my expectations, the more trustworthy the situation usually becomes. On the other hand, I can know and feel whether trust will ever be established and if not, I know to move away from it. I believe success is rarely achieved when trust is missing. I will not allow anyone I do not trust in close to me and if there are people I do not trust in my wider circle, I keep a watchful eye.

HEATHER SAYS
"TRUST IS WHAT HOLDS THINGS TOGETHER"

GIRLTALK CHALLENGE

The first step in Trust is making sure that you yourself are trustworthy - understanding what being a trustworthy person means and what that requires of you.

Make a list of situations in your life where you need to be a trustworthy person; then make a list of people who are depending on your trust.

Start with these lists and begin to establish and build the Trust factor, strengthening what you may already have in place. This will help you recognise your own expectations of TRUST in others.

Living Higher

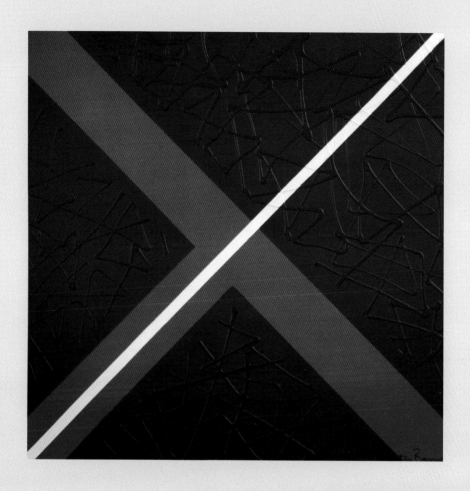

WISDOM

Be sure to apply wisdom at the crossroads

Full responsibility and ownership

Accept full responsibility for your life. The responsibility actually belongs to you, no-one else. Regardless of what happens to us, how we respond is ultimately up to us, even when it seems unfair and difficult.

When you do this, you quickly realise you have the ability to make positive changes. You hold the power to change your life. When women take full responsibility for themselves they begin a journey of powerful change. Accept responsibility for your circumstance and see life as the first step in the path of positive change. You no longer play the 'blame game' which holds you in a place of inaction. Playing the 'blame game' becomes an excuse for not taking responsibility. We must stop blaming others for the choices we ourselves have made.

When you take responsibility for your choices, you begin to choose more wisely, understanding you (no one else) will be accountable for the outcome. This is actually exciting news, because it means you are in charge of what happens.

Do not be afraid to take full responsibility and ownership of your life. The longer you avoid it, the more miserable and powerless you feel. Full responsibility sets you free to make your own decisions and make positive change so you can direct your own life. Full responsibility is very empowering. It is also the mature thing to do. Let's all grow up and get with the 'Full Responsibility and Ownership Programme'.

Own your own life, be responsible for it and begin to see you are very capable of making decisions for yourself and it will bring you much joy to see your life improve by your own choices. (Girls, I am not talking about marriage; regarding marital matters, ALL things include your husband.)

Make sure when you get to the end of your life you yourself have been responsible for the life you lived.

Personal Comment:

I believe your life is never going to be what you want it to be until you take responsibility for and ownership of it. I understand there are many reasons why people do not take responsibility and ownership for their own choices and lives. I suspect the crossing over from childhood to adulthood didn't take place properly, or maybe you have not yet stepped into your own power and authority, but I know it is NEVER too late to take full responsibility and ownership of your life. If you have not done so yet, do it now.

"One of the greatest feelings in life is the conviction that you have lived the life you wanted to live – with the rough and the smooth, the good and the bad – but yours, shaped by your own choices, and not someone else's."

MICHAEL IGNATIEFF[3]

Heather says "Own your own life"

GIRLTALK CHALLENGE

If you are an adult, please ask yourself "Am I taking responsibility for my own actions and choices?" If not, it's time to do so.

Start with one thing you are not happy with. Begin to make some decisions to change it.

Remember you are responsible for your own happiness.

MY MIRACLE
I painted this in thanks for receiving my miracle in 2006

The importance of wisdom in your decision making

Take your time when making important decisions.

Make sure you have gathered all the information and facts required (seek experienced counsel if required) to make informed decisions for the short and long term. Every decision needs consideration, even the smallest ones.

Wisdom covers bringing together several factors into decision making: knowledge, experience, understanding, common sense, discernment and insight.

- Deliberate carefully and consider all things. Have the ability to view things from a neutral perspective. Weigh pros and cons with an honest view, leaving out hype and emotion.
- Do not go ahead with decisions until you are sure you have all the bases covered.
- Make yourself fully aware of the areas of risk and pitfalls. If in doubt don't do it.
- Have a clear view of your path ahead.
- Know that very seldom is an impulsive decision successful.

If you slow down the decision-making process, you give time for unknown factors to surface. I find that very often when considering carefully a decision, then waiting for a period of time, more information will come my way to help confirm my decision or save me from making a mistake. Never be in too much of a hurry when important decisions are to be made. Use wisdom in all things.

Wisdom[16]: the ability to think and act utilising knowledge, experience, understanding, common sense, insight.

Wisdom shows us the way to making better choices. Before making an important decision, consider these questions carefully:

• Do I have all the information and facts required?
• What is my experience in this situation?
• Do I fully understand all the aspects of the situation that require consideration?
• Have I added common sense to the equation?
• Do I have some insight into the future and where this decision might take me?

Always pause and consider carefully at the crossroads. A wise woman is patient until she is certain.

Solomon was the wisest man ever to live; when asked what he wanted in life he said "Wisdom". Solomon's wisest choice was to request wisdom. Wisdom is supreme. Wisdom will enable you to look beneath the surface and discern the truth. Wisdom will help you look and see beyond what is in front of you.

"Wisdom is the principle thing, therefore get wisdom"

PROVERBS 4:7[5]

Personal Comment:

I'm not sure wisdom always comes with age – I believe some people never understand or have wisdom. I notice some people learn a little along the way; others develop it carefully and some just have an instinct for it. But I am sure by applying the basic principles – knowledge, experience, understanding, common sense and insight – to your decision-making, you won't go too far wrong.

One thing I have learnt is wisdom never rushes in…wisdom waits patiently.

I have also come to believe wisdom has a voice – if you wait and listen, you will hear wisdom speak to you, because wisdom wants you to do the right thing, make the right decision and succeed in all you do.

Wisdom is my dear friend and I never want to lose her. I want her to stay close to me at all times.

Heather says
"Listen to what wisdom is saying to you"

GIRLTALK CHALLENGE

Next time you have an important decision to make, apply wisdom.

Carefully gather and consider knowledge, experience, understanding, common sense and insight.

Don't rush in.

Gather information and get good advice.

Unwise decisions are costly on many levels.

Financial discipline

Money plays an enormous part in our lives and it is something we need to have firm control over, whether we like it or not. It has an enormous impact on our daily lives, so is an area requiring respect and good management.

It is important not to see money as the enemy, but as your friend. Your attitude towards money is relevant to how you manage it. Money is not evil – it is the misuse of it that creates problems.

- The biggest mistake some women make is turning a blind eye to their own spending. They do not have a budget and if they do, they often do not stick with it. Control over your finances is important.
- Inform yourself and get experienced advice with your budgeting. If someone else is doing this for you, keep yourself informed with the facts regularly. Stay connected to your finances.

Keep a very close watch on your spending and your financial position. This will help keep you in control of your finances – and therefore your life.

Have a written budget in a safe place and refer to it frequently.

- It is important to know what you are spending daily or weekly.
- Some women don't know what they spend each day or each week, or even monthly. Some are afraid to take an honest look, so when the bills roll in they spin out and sometimes go into denial.
- Overspending leads to major problems – not only financially, but with stress, health and relationships.
- Always follow a budget, carefully keeping check on your spending.
- Control your finances; don't let your finances control you.
- Living within your means gives you freedom and peace of mind.
- It is very empowering to know every detail of your living cost and to be in control of it.

- Don't give in to impulsive spending just to treat yourself when you feel low. (Visit a friend for a coffee instead.) You will buy things you definitely don't need, usually spending money you don't have, then end up having buyer's remorse and stressing about it.
- Impulse spending can give you a quick buzz, then a terrible low when the credit card account arrives.
- Don't be persuaded by advertising and 'good deals'. Nothing is a good deal if you don't need it and you are buying on impulse. Don't be vulnerable to advertising. Some women have a weakness in this area. Some women have emotional spending habits the same as emotional over eating - get help if you cannot control this. Stay away from shopping if you are emotional or upset.
- Some women have a particularly hard time with this at certain times of the month. Again recognise it and firmly take control of it. Make a choice not to go shopping.
- Have a good savings plan and don't break it.
- Save a little amount regularly to feel a little more secure about tomorrow.
- Don't spend tomorrow's income or prosperity.
- Break the cycle of spending tomorrow's income, because this will leave you feeling trapped and powerless in the area of finances.
- Don't cheat yourself of financial freedom tomorrow by overspending today.

This area of our lives has an enormous amount of control over us, more than some of us are aware of. However, we can manage our finances in such a way that it does not take over completely and spoil other areas of our life.

It is a fact that we, as a nation, are spending more than we are earning. The problems this causes and the consequences on health, relationships and families are enormous. We need to wise up. Let's forget about 'keeping up with the Joneses' and reduce our spending to within our means.

Spending more than you earn will come back to bite you. In the end don't deceive yourself into thinking it will all come right. Your chances of winning a lottery are slim!

66

Personal Comment:

I was brought up in a home where there wasn't a lot of money and certainly not for 'extras', but my mother had incredible budgeting skills! She seemed to be able to make a little go a very long way. She taught us well in this area.

I have a huge amount of respect for money and what it represents in my life. To the best of my ability, I endeavour to be a good steward of what I have been blessed with. But I do know, somewhere, on some level our attitude towards money plays a part in our prosperity (as well as hard work of course).

I believe money gives us options and so when we waste it or spend it thoughtlessly, we reduce our options in other areas. Even though I have been blessed financially in latter years, I still consider my options carefully every time I open my wallet.

I am not mean with money; in fact, I count it an honour to help someone financially – and I do whenever I think it appropriate – but I want to plant my finances in fertile ground, not throw money into a bottomless hole.

I urge you to consider where your money is going.

Heather says
"Respect your finances and they will serve you well"

99

GIRLTALK CHALLENGE

If you do not have a weekly or monthly budget for your spending, I recommend you get one ASAP!

Find someone to help you with this.

Most of all, stick to it and enjoy seeing what happens to your financial situation.

Believe in your God-given dreams

Your life is significant and there is a purpose to be fulfilled. Believe in yourself to achieve the dreams in your heart. You will find your true purpose deeply written in your heart. You have been born for something magnificent.

Develop a strong and deep belief in yourself and your potential. Do not doubt for a moment you have an ability to make your dreams happen - you absolutely do! Whatever your dream requires, you have the ability for it.

Have complete confidence and know, by having a plan and executing it well, you can achieve your God-given dream. In fact there is no reason it cannot happen, it's just a matter of making all the right choices and having patience and determination to see it through. Your God-given dream is probably the reason you were born, and why you are here at this time.

Align yourself with people who encourage and motivate you, people who will not destroy your dream but contribute to it. Be wary of people who will want to kill your dream. There are many of these people around. (I have certainly met a few of these on my journey.)

In the initial stages of developing your dream, consider carefully how many people to share it with. You may be disappointed to find not everyone you tell will want you to be successful. Don't be in too much of a hurry to tell everyone; wait for the appropriate time when you are well on your way, to reduce the risk of interference from the wrong people and the dream being destroyed.

- Protect your dream fiercely. It may be the very reason you were born.
- Know your life is significant and you deserve to achieve all you know you can.
- Everyone has the right and the ability to dream a dream, and fulfil it. You have to choose it, step into it. Put the right choices behind the dream and see it unfold.
- Have a detailed plan and a timeframe in which you want to have achieved your dream. (Be reasonable, often our dreams take longer than we anticipate.)
- Get whatever advice and assistance you need, from the right people, to help you along the way.
- Celebrate the small successes along the way and eventually you will achieve your dream.

DON'T GIVE UP. HANG IN THERE. BE PERSISTENT.
KEEP BELIEVING.

Seeing your dreams fulfilled is one of life's greatest pleasures. Even the smallest of dreams is hugely significant. Don't underestimate small dreams. Every dream has an equal right to be fulfilled.

Personal Comment:

I am a firm believer of the saying "Dreams do come true if you really want them to!" The question is…Are you prepared to do what your dream requires of you, for it to be fulfilled? Everyone has a dream, but might not admit it or even realise it. I believe it's part of being born into the world.

As I see it, the only difference between people who achieve their dreams and those who don't, is those who don't achieve them, don't want them badly enough to do whatever it takes. Maybe they have trouble believing in them because they lack faith. I guess it's different for different people, but I know for sure dreams do come true if you really really really want them to! Find out why you are not living your dreams.

Dream your dreams and keep them alive until you achieve them.

Writing this book has been one of my dreams – it's in its sixth year of making! I haven't given up on it! As each year goes by, I add a little more of myself and my understanding to it.

When I was a child I had a lot of dreams of a better life for myself; dreams of doing something great for others; dreams of making contributions to change people's lives forever; dreams for my family; dreams for my financial success and many more. I can honestly say I have achieved all of my childhood dreams and I am now working on my adult dreams, taking my dreams to a higher level than I ever thought possible. Give yourself permission to believe in your dreams and live them.

HEATHER SAYS
"DREAMS DO COME TRUE, IF YOU REALLY
WANT THEM TO"

GIRLTALK CHALLENGE

Discover the Dream in Your Heart. You may have a number of them, that's great!

Identify the ONE that seems most important to you - the one you would choose if you were granted One Wish. The one that makes your heart beat faster, when you think about it.

Once you have discovered it, WRITE IT DOWN. Next write a list of things and people you would need to achieve it.

Clarify it in your mind and BELIEVE in it.

Positive thinking and awesome attitudes

Positive thinking is powerful in our lives. What we think, powerfully impacts our lives. It is possible to control what we think and change our attitudes.

Focusing our minds to think positively takes practice, requires discipline and a strong belief in ourselves and what we want to achieve. It also requires understanding that you are responsible for your 'thoughts'.

- Identifying negative thought requires a conscious effort to recognise what's going on in your 'thought life'. Listen carefully to your thoughts and you will quickly discover whether you are a positive or negative thinker. (Apparently a high percentage of our thoughts are negative. Check yours out; you may be surprised!)
- Identify negative thoughts, eliminate them and replace with positive thoughts immediately
- Example: I can't solve this problem → Every problem has a solution. I will find it, or someone to help me with the solution → This problem will be solved to my satisfaction
- Example: This is impossible → This is possible, I will give it more focus, time and energy and I will accomplish this. There is a solution to every problem; I just need to find the solution! Nothing is impossible! When you believe there is a solution to your problem, you open the door for it to make its way to you.
- Worry is negative thought. Worrying doesn't achieve anything but it does get you down and saps your energy. Perception is most often worse than reality. You do have the power to alter your thinking; you can control your mind and not let your mind control you.
- Establish a firm belief that great things are happening to you and for you; the outcome of all things in your life will be positive. Establish this belief, then change how you view things, which will then change the decisions or choices you make, which will change your actions - resulting in a better outcome.
- Think and speak positive things into your life, it will make a difference!

Develop a mental attitude to back yourself all the way. "I really do deserve the best!" "The best things do happen for me."

- Worry and stress usually come from negative thinking; change the way you think about a situation and you have taken the first step to actually changing the situation itself. When you take positive action your worry and stress level decrease.

Don't allow your thoughts to become loose and wander into negative, destructive thinking. Be honest about how much time is spent in negative thought. Recognise negative thought for what it is and change it immediately. Press the delete button in your mind as if it was your computer. Don't let your mind entertain negative thinking. I have discovered our minds will automatically go to the negative, so we need to pause and change negative thinking to the positive. This is a habit we can break.

Take the time to THINK about what it is you are THINKING about. Be sure you know what it is you are thinking about and what is controlling your thoughts. Focus on the good things in your life and build on them. A few years ago an advertising agency placed advertisements in newspapers calling us all to "Eliminate the negative, accentuate the positive". I have not forgotten this and believe it was great advice to us as a nation.

Mentally picture success and positive things in your life and develop an attitude to come into line with your positive thoughts. Positive actions then follow and positive results are the outcome.

Think positive and empowering thoughts. Take control over your thinking - conquer this and you will enjoy your life more.

Speak something positive, and do something positive, to reinforce your positive and powerful attitude. You will experience a powerful phenomenon; it will become addictive, you will see results. When we allow positive thinking to dominate our minds, these things will eventually be seen in our life if we keep an unshakable belief in ourselves and our future. It changes our attitudes and 'our attitude determines our altitude'.

Our thoughts can either help or hurt us; we choose. Don't allow your negative thinking to destroy your life and your enjoyment. Take control at this moment to eliminate any negative thoughts which may be entering as you are reading this - there may be a part of you rejecting what you are reading. That is your choice. Remember, you own your thoughts.

Take ownership of your thoughts and have powerful, positive thoughts which will lead to having an awesome attitude, which in turn leads to a powerful and positive life. It's all in the choice you make. Believe it, you can do it.

Be a positive thinker and develop an awesome attitude and you will most definitely go to a higher altitude. When you focus on the positive in all situations, it's almost as if you'll get caught in an upward draught to take you higher in life.

People can say positive things, but be thinking negatively. That's why our thoughts and spirits must have the same intention. Our thoughts determine the direction we take. For example, if we are controlled by fear, but we do not recognise it, we will make decisions based on the negative aspect of fear, even when we may be actually speaking positively. Your innermost thoughts and intentions need to be in agreement with what you are saying and doing.

We will never reach our potential by negative, fearful thinking. It will hold us back every step of the way. It will set us on the wrong path. On the other hand, I discovered replacing negative thought with positive thought begins a whole different journey in that particular circumstance. You can turn events by changing your attitude and being more positive.

Being thankful for what you have, the position you are in and the opportunities still available will open doors for you.

PERSONAL COMMENT:

I can't remember exactly when I started to get this revelation of listening to my thoughts and engaging for a moment to really hear whether they were negative or positive, but I can tell you it was a number of years ago.

I started simply - every time I realised I had thought something negative, I spoke aloud something positive to negate it and eliminate its power. It took a while to break the negative habit and develop a new positive habit of thinking good things. I understood my negative thinking came from my past and made me expect negative things to happen.

I have spent the more recent years disciplining my mind to think positively and developing a positive attitude of gratitude for all I am blessed with, being grateful and thankful every day for the little things.

I am now open to the very best life I can have. I believe I deserve it and it is mine to have – if I choose to have positive and grateful thoughts, words and actions, use encouraging words and move in supportive action. I believe our thoughts do determine what we create in our life, so let's work on our thought life!

I personally use the Inspired Word of God (the Bible) to speak over negative situations. I personally believe the Word of God carries the Power of God into the situation and changes it. This has been the truth in my life.

"Be transformed by the renewing of your mind"
ROMANS 12:2[8]

HEATHER SAYS
"CLEAN UP YOUR THOUGHT LIFE"

GIRLTALK CHALLENGE

Think of your mind and your thoughts like a computer. Think of negative thought like spam, and delete it the moment you recognise it.

Replace it with something positive, pleasing and productive for yourself and others. Practise, practise, practise and you will begin to feel the upward draught lifting you higher!

The power of the spoken word

The power of every word we speak out of our mouth, does one of two things: Encourages and edifies or discourages and destroys. Wow! This can be frightening!

If we realised the power and impact of our words, I believe we would be disappointed when we think back to some of the things we have said to people, particularly the ones we love. However, most things (not all, so be careful) can be undone with sincere words of apology and regret.

A critical, negative word into someone's life can have a long-term devastating effect on that person. Do we want to be remembered for something like that? Surely we want to be remembered for saying something positive and encouraging which changed someone's life for the better.

- If you don't have anything encouraging to say, perhaps you shouldn't say anything.
- Women must understand the power of the spoken word; it has the power to be life giving or life taking.
- Remember once it is out there, you can't take it back.

The power of the spoken word has the potential to produce success or failure in people's lives.

- Don't be fooled into thinking you must say something negative or hurtful, even when you sincerely believe you are right on the matter - although you have the right to defend yourself, or put a stop to someone else's negative impact on your life.
- Check your attitude before bringing a difficult situation into discussion.
- Even a difficult situation can be turned into a positive, encouraging experience for all concerned when handled with sensitivity and with a good attitude.
- Always end a discussion by speaking encouragement and affirmation.

Personal Comment:

I can honestly say I am disappointed with myself for some of the things I have said over the years out of anger, frustration or hurt. In fact, I shudder at how I may have hurt others with my words. Sometimes I have spoken angrily without thinking, especially when I myself was hurting. One of the things I have learnt to do in these situations is apologise quickly. Even when I believe I am in the right, I still apologise for causing hurt. I make sure I articulate something good back into the situation where possible.

It brings peace to my soul and as I get older I really want peace and goodness in my life. I am not too proud to apologise to anyone to achieve this. I urge you to discipline yourself to always find something good to say in every situation. Remember – we reap what we sow, even with words.

I have realised my life is valuable and time is short, so I encourage us all to think before we speak.

The words "I love you" are very powerful. Use them generously with the people you truly love.

HEATHER SAYS
"A LOVING WORD IS A LIFE-GIVING WORD"

GIRLTALK CHALLENGE

Make a point of telling the people you love "I Love You" on a regular basis.

The more love you give out, the more will return to you.

Make a deal with yourself from now on, when speaking (even when dealing with difficult situations) to end a discussion with a positive encouraging word.

SUNRISE TO SUNSET
Sing from sunrise to sunset

Service above self

- Develop an attitude of service, not self, by thinking of ways to help others before thinking about your own needs.
- Have a serving attitude and let it come from your heart naturally.
- Put others first. This should just happen naturally without thought or discussion (as most mothers do with their children).
- Know by serving others, you learn about yourself. Serving others is much more satisfying and pleasurable than attending to yourself.
- Service over self will take you to a higher altitude and you will live on a different plane than those who put themselves first. There is a very large gap between self first and service first. Actually it's enormous.
- Service above self is applicable to any position you have in life; in fact the higher you go, the more you serve. Service above self will gain you natural promotion, in order for you to serve others in a greater way.
- It seems to be the natural order of things. There are certain natural laws which override anything we can achieve. When we live in service above self, it seems a phenomenon takes place to lift you higher than you could possibly go yourself. This is an exciting and rewarding place to be.
- Putting others first comes from a confidence in your own position.
- Putting others first always makes you the winner in every situation.

Have an attitude and belief which goes beyond yourself. Know connecting with others for the good of others is what will and can change our world. In doing so you will dramatically change your world in ways I cannot even begin to describe – but believe me "it's all good!"

Compassion for those less fortunate

Please, girls, have compassion for those less fortunate than you. It is so important to remember not everyone is as fortunate as you are. Allow yourself to be deeply moved by the plight of others and be mobilised into action. Whenever you have the capacity to help others, do so. Don't hesitate; you really don't need time to think about it. Helping those less fortunate can be as natural as breathing. Every small thing helps a great deal more than we realise.

If you see a need close to you and you are in a position to meet it – maybe it is meant to be your responsibility. (Being sensible and using common sense of course!)

Know even the little things can make a big difference in someone's life, so go out of your way to do these small things. Have eyes to see another's pain or feel their sorrow. Show love and understanding to others and have the ability to bridge gaps between ourselves and those less fortunate.

- Don't be a person who would only move in your own circle of comfort, but become a person who extends yourself to the wider community in our society and beyond.
- Have a heart that beats for others. The motivation and compassion to make a difference is a rewarding and fulfilling experience like no other. Reach out to someone today!
- We are blessed to be a blessing. Use some of your blessing to bless someone less fortunate.
- It's better to give than to receive. It really is! This is not just a cliché.
- Giving is a privilege, because it means if you are in a position to give, then you are a blessed person indeed.

As we all know, there are people around us and in the world, who do not have enough for basic needs for life for themselves, let alone have something to give others. Meeting someone else's need is one of the GREATEST PRIVILEGES AND PLEASURES in LIFE. Don't let greed or selfishness cheat you out of this amazing gift you have. Open your compassionate heart to give – make it a priority, make it a lifestyle.

Be a generous giver

- Being a generous person means constantly thinking of ways you can give to others and help others.
- Being very aware of meeting the needs of others is something a generous person does naturally.
- Being a natural gift giver will mean you often sacrifice for yourself to give to others.
- Your pleasure and delight is in making others happy or fulfilling a need they have.
- Generous people have a beautiful open hand and heart at all times.
- You can become one of these people; start by giving something of yourself every day to another person e.g. your time, attention, consideration, love or compassion; by baking a cake, sending a card, flowers, text or e-mail. Generosity takes shape in many ways. It doesn't have to cost you financially - often the best expression of generosity is your time and love.
- Make a conscious effort to extend yourself beyond your own need on a daily basis. Your effort just could be the difference in someone's day or life.
- Know the difference between being a giver and allowing others to take from you.
- Be wary of people who subtly suggest you should 'give'. Some people are very good at manipulating others into giving to them. (This is really taking.)
- A naturally generous giver gives more (and more often) than most other people. Their generosity shines out!

Generosity is indeed a beautiful gift when it comes from the heart and it speaks volumes when displayed gracefully and discreetly. Boasting about one's generosity shows the giver is not coming from a true generous heart - if she is looking for credit, or recognition.

Sometimes generosity is rarely seen, but for sincere generous people it's as natural as breathing. It comes from a beautiful spirit and will make you feel complete. This does not mean you have to give everything away.

True generosity is a God-given gift – cherish it and enjoy it.

Personal Comment:

When I thought about what were my heart's desires and what was at the core of my dreams, it was always connected to serving others, helping others, supporting others, encouraging others and helping others to have a better life in any way I can. Actually I think it's possibly at the heart of most people (I hope it is) but so often other things in our life get in the way of us doing what is really in our hearts.

I believe sacrifice and reward go hand in hand. It appears to me to be another one of those natural laws like sowing and reaping.

Looking back over the situations where I made sacrifice for others, always an unexpected and delightful reward came my way. I certainly don't do things for others expecting a reward; in fact, it never enters my mind, but I am aware that when I sacrifice something of myself to benefit others, I am rewarded in many wonderful ways. It's true that we can't out give God – He is the Greatest Giver of all.

In recent years, my heart has begun to literally ache for those less fortunate than I am. I see myself as hugely privileged in life and I am now beginning to understand the responsibility I have, to do what I can do to assist those who don't have life basic essentials to maintain their dignity. We can make excuses and say "Well, it's their choice". That is true in some cases, but in many other situations they don't have a choice at all, or they are not able to make the right one at present. Let us not forget that any one of us could find ourselves in this position at any time; we do not know what lies ahead of us. Extend your hand a little each day.

I believe meeting the needs of others is the reason for my existence. Surely my existence in the world could not be to meet my own need only. I give when I feel moved in my heart to give, not when someone else suggests it, or hoping for acceptance or approval from others. That is not the true spirit of generosity.

I am sure you, like me, find generosity a very rewarding experience. Most often when I feel 'moved' to give, I will meet someone's profound need. At these times I know I have been used by God to help someone and something bigger than I will ever know takes place.

I heard someone say at the Women's International 'Colour' Conference, in Sydney 2007,

> "To the world you may seem like one person, but to that one person you may seem like the world."

It went directly into the centre of my heart and moved me.

HEATHER SAYS
"TRUE GENEROSITY MOVES THE HEART — IN SERVING OTHERS YOU WILL FIND YOUR OWN JOY"

———————————————— 99 ————————————————

Girltalk Challenge

Make a decision today to make a sacrifice for someone else. Allow your heart to be moved so you are prompted to be generous to that person and put their needs before your own.

The next time you are about to do something for yourself – perhaps treat yourself in some way - instead do it for someone else.

God is always waiting for someone to display a generous heart. He will show you just the right person for you to bless. Choose someone in need and notice the surprise they get from what you do for them. It will be like a gift from heaven for them. How beautiful is that!

Ask yourself "Did I get a bigger buzz from that than if I'd done it for myself?" Take a blessing in your life and give it to someone who would appreciate it.

Perhaps step outside your world of comfort and step inside the world of someone less fortunate than you. Show some of that compassion I know you have inside of you.

Just do it, girls!

Beauty surrounds us

Develop a detailed eye for the beauty in all things and allow the beauty you see to far outweigh anything else in your view. Train your mind and your eye to prioritise absorbing the most beautiful things around you. Take delight in them.

I believe taking just a moment out of a busy schedule to acknowledge and give thanks for the most beautiful things in your life can have a greater impact on you than you might realise. Recognising beauty is a very pleasurable pastime – and only takes a few moments! These moments can and will be the best part of your day. God's creation never fails to move people who see it for what it really is and all its beauty.

Viewing the beauty around you will bring so much joy into your heart. Connect not only with creation but with God the creator, as you acknowledge the beauty of His creation. Some people miss this amazing gift by being too busy to notice.

There is beauty in everything and everyone when you narrow your view to focus only on the beauty. Recognising this as a reality and truth in your life is a powerful experience. It will change how you live your life and how you see the world. When you do not recognise on a daily basis, the beautiful world you live in, you miss out on so much.

In addition to your eyes seeing the beauty, take the time to let the beauty of what you see penetrate deep within you. That is connection with nature, where you become one with Creation and the Creator. That indeed is a wonderful moment.

Personal Comment:

I find beautiful things feed my soul and make me want to sing with joy. It can be anything from nature, to architecture, to music and people.

I am continually searching with my eyes and my heart to see and hear beautiful things so I can take a moment to admire and enjoy.

I find this very pleasurable and it feeds my creativity. Life and people really are beautiful and I am frequently overwhelmed by the privilege of having a beautiful life, surrounded by such magnificence. However, I am mindful the beauty I see is something I deliberately search for and seek out just for the pleasure of acknowledging it and being part of it. In doing that, I allow the beauty of what I see to become part of me.

Heather says
"See the beauty that surrounds you"

Girltalk Challenge

Stop right now and look around, test your eye to see the beauty around you. This takes discipline and practice but once you have trained your eye for the beautiful, it changes the view of your world and the people in it.

Stop! Look out the window
Stop! Look at your child
Stop! Look at the water
Stop! Look at the colour
Stop! Look at the trees

Notice the shape, the sparkle, the smile, the movement, the smell, the sound, the touch, the stillness, the breeze.

There is so much beauty surrounding you wherever you are. Choose to see it and it will move you, change you and bless you.

RENEWAL

The wonder of nature renews itself

You are creative

Everyone of us has a share of creativity. I believe we were all born with a creative gift, or artistic talent. Each and every one of us has something unique inside that can be released through creative expression.

Each creative gift is different for every single person. Your creative gift is unique and special to you. Find that beautiful part of you that is tucked away inside, if you haven't already discovered it.

Some people have many creative gifts and others have one or two in particular. Creativity can be expressed in many ways, the more obvious ones being writing, painting, music, song, sculpting, gardening, floral art, designing, decorating etc.

However, your creative gift may be something entirely different, but it will be valuable because everyone's gift is different and unique, but equally precious.

Art comes in limitless forms, and there is no right or wrong, it's ART. It's an expression of something or someone. Expressing your creative gift in most cases will be one of the most joyous things you will do. That's how you know it's your gift from God, for the purpose of sharing it. A creative gift that is held captive and not released will cause frustration and even depression in some situations.

You were born to be creative! Take time to find and explore your creative gift or gifts; they will help you 'to fly'. Make it a priority to be involved with your creative gift regularly. It's an important and beautiful part of who you are.

Personal Comment:

I never thought of myself as being creative until I was in my 40s. My creative gifts were stifled somewhat, by career, family, businesses and what I thought were more demanding interests. Now and again they got loose, but I didn't recognise them until I gave them time and allowed them to expand.

I discovered my love of painting quite by surprise, almost three years ago. I decided to give all my family members a painting as a joke Christmas gift. They would not have considered me artistic; in fact I didn't consider myself an artist. I bought budget canvases and paints and began to splash paint around as a bit of fun, to create a painting for each person. I discovered an enormous amount of pleasure and of 'release' of something inside of me that was longing and waiting for an opportunity to express itself. It was as if my soul was waiting to dance and I had given it the freedom and the platform to do so.

I have continued to paint; in fact I now cannot stop; it has become a vital part of my communication to the world. I have included some of my paintings in this book, as another way of communicating with you.

Another thing I have discovered about my creative gifts is they 'heal' my emotions and keep me balanced. When I engage in creating something beautiful from within, it releases something that has goodness attached to it.

Once you begin to indulge yourself in your gift, you may discover, as I have, many other gifts and talents begin to emerge. Creativity expands as you use it. The more time you give it, the more it grows. Then you begin to surprise yourself – and it's fun. I CAN, YOU CAN, WE CAN!

Heather says
"Set your creative gifts free"

GIRLTALK CHALLENGE

Discover your creative gifts.

Think about one thing you love to do which makes you feel calm and good about yourself – it could possibly be one of your creative gifts.

Spend some time doing that very thing in the next few days and begin to notice how you 'feel' while you are doing it and after you have finished.

Once you are sure you know what your special gift or gifts might be, make them a priority in your life. They will add a richness and fulfilment other things will not give you.

CREATION

The magnificent colour of creation

Making your house a home

Women express themselves in the houses they live in. You have the ability to create a wonderful home for your family and friends. Yes, you do - take the time to apply what you instinctively know - we have a homemaking instinct within us like the nesting instinct.

Consider ways to make your house a home, with attention to detail. You can be creative in your home without it costing you a lot of money e.g. candles, flowers, soaps, towels, pictures, photographs, music and smells. Most of us have these things available in our homes; it's the attention and focus you give them which make the difference.

Again, it's thought, words and actions which can produce a wonderful feeling of love and after all, that's what people respond to – the atmosphere, to feel welcome, safe and nurtured; to feel loved. When you are in a home that has love, you will feel at HOME. 'Being Loved' is like a 'coming home' feeling.

Homes that are clean, tidy and have a sense of order about them are homes which are loved and looked after. Women who are relaxed and do not make a fuss, allow others to feel at ease in their home.

A home which is open, inviting, warm, colourful and full of love for all who enter is a wonderful place to visit and is often a place you don't want to leave. Your home is an expression of the people who live there but mostly, it's an expression of you, the 'Woman of the House'. Express yourself beautifully in Your Home. I am not talking about expensive furniture and décor, I am suggesting the little things that show and express you love and care for your family and friends.

Love towards others in our homes is one of the most important ingredients in making a wonderful home. People who are fortunate to live in a home where love is the predominant factor, have been given a beautiful gift and are incredibly blessed. Each of us has the opportunity wherever we are, with whatever kind of home we live in, to create an atmosphere of love, worth, welcome and nurturing - the most important ingredients to making a wonderful home.

Take pride in your home. Keep it well presented and cared for - this is also a reflection of love, so people will be drawn to the warmth and welcome of your home. Having a home people like to visit and feel comfortable in, reflects well on you.

66

PERSONAL COMMENT:

I have had to grow into this because for many years I was extremely busy with working and building a business with my husband, so I neglected to make my house a home. Yes, it was always clean and orderly, but I didn't take time to add my expression to it.

However, now I take great pleasure in making our house feel like a home, and have people feel they can drop in at any time and feel welcome. I like people to come in and make their own coffee – they don't have to wait to be asked, they feel at home in my house. Sit down, relax, put your feet up – yes, put your feet up! My friends frequently take their shoes off and put their feet up on the sofa, I do the same – then we chat and laugh together.

I want people to feel special when they visit. I want them to feel loved and cared for and to leave my home feeling happier than when they arrived.

HEATHER SAYS
'LOVE IS THE ESSENTIAL INGREDIENT
FOR HOMEMAKING'

GIRLTALK CHALLENGE

Walk around the main area of your house, and look for ways to make it more homely. How you can apply your LOVE to it?

Maybe you just need to have a rearrange of things to brighten and freshen it up. Maybe just by purchasing a few extra 'bits and pieces' you can change your house into a much loved home.

It doesn't have to be a costly exercise, but pieces added with love can add much to a home's real value.

Making your
house a home
with the
simple things

An attitude of gratitude

You may have heard the saying "An attitude of gratitude will determine your altitude". I personally have found this to be true in my life; turning your focus to the things you are thankful for and away from the things that have been difficult.

I like to start each new day with thanksgiving. Being thankful for what the day ahead will bring. Having a positive expectancy. Being thankful for all I have available to me to meet my needs.

Try it – have a thankful expectation of what is ahead. Say 'Thank you' in advance. Walk into a new day giving thanks so it will change what you will attract to yourself.

I also believe it's important to end the day with thanksgiving, regardless of what the day brought. Be thankful for all the things that happened, because they reminded you today you are indeed ALIVE and tomorrow will be another wonderful day of opportunity. A God-given Opportunity. For we are here by the grace of God.

Whatever your circumstance, find something in it to be thankful for; to express your gratitude for the opportunity to learn and grow and become better. I believe you move towards that which you think about, so keeping your attitude full of thankfulness could draw you to more experiences and happenings to give thanks for.

You may be thinking 'it's very hard to do that', if you are going through a difficult time, but I have discovered when you turn your attention to the things you are grateful for, you move toward more of that, and away from the negative. So take control of your thinking, start with small things e.g. thank you for my family; thank you for my job; thank you for my health; thank you for my home; thank you for the opportunity.

It takes making a conscious choice to do this, regardless of what you feel about it. Just do it and I am sure you will notice a change begin to happen.

66

Personal Comment:

I have personally discovered the measure of gratitude I feel is directly linked to the measure of joy I feel. So if I am feeling a little low, I begin to say out loud all the things I am grateful for - "Count my Blessings" in other words. In a very short time, I am full of Joy. This really does work – try it. Make it a daily habit. I believe this is the biggest gift you can give yourself.

I have learned and disciplined myself to be in an attitude of gratitude almost continually, in all things at all times. Yes, it took a huge effort because I too have many things in my life I could choose not to be grateful for, but I was determined I was no longer going to give those things my time and thoughts so they could bring me down.

Instead I focus on all the things I am grateful for and keep my attention on those things. This is now a natural inclination for me and has changed my life, my health, my opportunities, my future.

"There is not a more pleasing exercise of the mind than gratitude." **JOSEPH ADDISON**[17]

HEATHER SAYS "JUST BE GRATEFUL"

GIRLTALK CHALLENGE

Make a list of the top ten things you are grateful for. Make it a priority to focus on those at the beginning and end of each day (and in between times too if you remember).

Watch how your attitude to your life will begin to change.

THANK YOU! THANK YOU! THANK YOU!
Being thankful in all things

Be spiritually connected

We are so much more than most of us can comprehend. We are not just a body and a mind. I believe most people know this deep down in their innermost being. Unless we have good sound explanations reminding us we are indeed a spirit with significant purpose, we can flounder, lost and alone all of our lives.

We are indeed a Body, Soul and Spirit as previously mentioned in this book. To be spiritually connected, is to be connected to God, the Creator of Heaven and Earth – and that includes us!

God created us to be connected to Him in spirit as He is connected to all His creations. He did not create us to then leave us alone. No way! However, the choice is ours, we can choose to believe He is indeed who He says He is, in His Inspired Word (The Bible), or we can choose not to believe. He does give us a choice – please choose God.

It's a wonderful thing to know God and let Him know you - to be in a relationship with Him, to be connected by your spirit to Him, to know all you are and you do goes way beyond you. To know your life is by the grace of God and not by anything you do or say, is a wonderful, liberating place to be; to know and to recognise all good things come from God, for He is 'Unconditional Love'.

To stay spiritually connected to this source of Unconditional Love gives life here on Earth a whole new meaning. Walk with God and be spiritually connected to Him. Carry the presence and peace of God with you.

When you spiritually connect with Him, He will look after you – for you are His creation and He cares for you deeply. Being spiritually connected with God brings enlightenment, for He is Light. He lights the way for us.

To be spiritually connected to God is to be complete in a way only found with God.

Personal Comment:

How do I know this? More than 25 years ago I discovered for myself that God was in fact who He said He was in His Inspired Word (The Bible), and when I connected with Him through Jesus Christ, my life began a journey of transformation that is almost unbelievable to me now.

I now know we must be spiritually connected to God to be part of the greater plan for our lives. Not only the greater plan, but the BEST POSSIBLE PLAN.

Through my journey as a Christian I have discovered much about myself and my reason for being alive. Although I am still learning, I do have a sense of peace and purpose through my faith. I have discovered I have nothing to fear and a lot to be excited about and to look forward to.

He never leaves me, He always answers when I call. It still completely overwhelms me to think God the Creator of Heaven and Earth actually speaks to me. He does and He helps me with all my decision-making, protects me and blesses me, just because I put Him at the top of my list. He is my most favourite person – I know without a doubt my life WOULD NOT look anything like it does today had I not discovered God through His Son, Jesus Christ. I make it a priority every day to stay Spiritually Connected to God through Jesus, my Lord and Saviour.

Jesus said "I am the Way, the Truth and the Life.
No one comes to the Father except through me" JOHN 14:6[B]

I know this to be the Truth of all Truths.

Please note – I am not talking about being religious, for I do not consider myself religious. I am talking about a relationship with God our Heavenly Father. If you want to be spiritually connected to God through Jesus Christ, then pray this prayer below with an honest and sincere heart and be blessed, my dear friend.

HEATHER SAYS
"GOD IS GREAT"

Dear Heavenly Father,
I am grateful you know me and love me.
Thank you for sending Jesus to die on the cross for me,
so I can believe in Him and receive the Gift of the Holy Spirit.
Thank you for saving me by your grace.
I ask you to forgive my sin.
I receive you as my Lord and Saviour.
Today I begin my new life with you.
Please guide me from this day forward so I may fulfil
my God-given Purpose.
In Jesus' name AMEN

GIRLTALK CHALLENGE

It's one thing to not do something because you do not know any better, but it's another choice altogether to do or not do something when you have been informed.

I trust you will consider carefully my section on "Being Spiritually Connected".

As I write this, I am praying for you to know the truth as I discovered it, to begin a wonderful life being spiritually connected to God, through His Son Jesus.

Be Blessed, Darling Girlfriend!

One more thing

Before you put this book down, I would like to say one more
thing – isn't that just like us, girls, we always have more to say…

> Be strong
> Stand firm
> Have faith

and time will turn in your favour.

This I know. If we do all the things we have "talked" about in the
past 52 chapters to the best of our ability, we will most definitely
be living a GREAT LIFE.

You may already know much of what I have written, but it is the
"**doing**", not the "**knowing**" where the GREAT LIFE is found.

Just do it girls!

THE VOICE OF MY HEART

Speaking from your heart brings truth

SHARE YOUR STORY...

From Heather:

I would love to hear your story. Now you've read this book, you may understand how your story could inspire or support another woman. I want to know about you and your life story.

In 1,000 words or fewer, please share your story. Tell me how you overcame a challenge or a difficult situation in your life.

Sharing your story with others will not only remind you of your learning and achievement, but will encourage and help liberate others from similar circumstances.

Your story is your treasure and it has tremendous value.

Tell your story on www.mygirltalkstory.com

REFERENCES

1- Dictionary.com. Dictionary.com Unabridged (v 1.1). Random House, Inc. http://dictionary.reference.com/browse/great

2- Dictionary.com. The American Heritage® Dictionary of the English Language, Fourth Edition. Houghton Mifflin Company, 2004. http://dictionary.reference.com/browse/wisdom Dictionary.com. Dictionary.com Unabridged (v 1.1). Random House, Inc. http://dictionary.reference.com/browse/wisdom

3- Ignatieff, M. (2004). *Living Fearlessly in a Fearful World.* Whitman Commencement Address, 2004. [Online]. Retrieved August 27, 2007, from http://www.whitman.edu/content/news/ LivingFearlesslyinaFearfulWorld

4- Dictionary.com. Dictionary.com Unabridged (v 1.1). Random House, Inc. http://dictionary.reference.com/browse/excellent Dictionary.com. WordNet® 3.0. Princeton University. http:// dictionary.reference.com/browse/excellence

5- Meyer, J. *Spirit, Soul and Body teaching series.* Available through www.joycemeyer.org

6- *Holy Bible.* New King James Version. (1982). Thomas Nelson Inc. Tennessee, USA.

7- Thesaurus.com. *Roget's New Millennium™ Thesaurus, First Edition* (v 1.3.1). Lexico Publishing Group, LLC. http://thesaurus. reference.com/browse/integrity

8- *Holy Bible.* New International Version. (1984). The Zondervan Corporation. Michigan, USA.

9- as quoted in *Live Good.* (2004). Compiled by Kobi Yamada. Compendium Publishing & Communications, Lynnwood, USA.

10- Winfrey, O. (2007, August). *'O' The Oprah Magazine*, Vol 8, No.8.

11- Thesaurus.com. *Roget's New Millennium™ Thesaurus*, First Edition (v 1.3.1). Lexico Publishing Group, LLC. http://thesaurus.reference.com/browse/expansion

12- Cloud, H., and Townsend, J. (1992) *Boundaries.* Zondervan Publishing. http://www.christianbook.com/Christian/Books/product?item_no=58590&event=1033SBFI30949I1033

13- Lorde, A. (2007, August). *'O' The Oprah Magazine*, Vol 8, No.8.

14- King, M. Retrieved September 5, 2007, from http://www.wisdomquotes.com/cat_service.html

15- Gray, J. (2003). *Men are from Mars, Women are from Venus.* Harper Collins Publishers.

16- *Collins Concise Dictionary,* 3rd Edition Revised 1995, Harper Collins Publishers.

17- Addison, J. Retrieved September 3, 2007, from www.quotegarden.com/gratitude.html